THE WHITE WOMAN AND HER VALLEY

Other Books by ARCH MERRILL

THE
WHITE WOMAN AND
AND
HER VALLEY

By *ARCH MERRILL*

Sixth Printing

Address all orders and inquiries to Creek Books, P.O. Box 9633, Rochester, N. Y. 14604.

Manufactured by American Book–Stratford Press, Inc., 75 Varick Street, New York, N. Y. 10013.

Contents

List of Illustrations

List of Illustrations

THE WHITE WOMAN AND HER VALLEY

Chapter 1

In This Valley

"In the green and silent valley,
By the pleasant water courses,
Spread the meadows and the corn fields,
And beyond them stood the forest. . . ."
From *The Song of Hiawatha*

———

No one has ever known the Genesee Valley without coming under its spell.

Aptly the Indians gave it the name of Genesee, which means in their tongue, "pleasant banks." Even the river keeps twisting and turning, looking backward, as if loath to leave its Valley.

"The green and silent valley" was the Eden of the Senecas, the once powerful Keepers of the Western Door of the Iroquois Long House. They knew every turn, every mood of the northward flowing river that begins in the Pennsylvania mountains and ends in marriage with the inland sea called Ontario. Along the pleasant banks ran their trails worn smooth by many moccasined feet.

Dear to Indian hearts was the broad and fertile Valley. There nature had left openings in the oak forest. There

3

the hills rolled back gently from the meandering river. There grew the finest corn and beans and squash.

Untutored yet sensitive to beauty, the Red Men thrilled to the majesty of a masterpiece of the Great Spirit, the mighty green-gray canyon of the Genesee, in which thundered the three falls of Portage, the carrying place for the war canoes.

When the paleface colonists rose in rebellion against the English crown, the Senecas lost their Eden forever. Into the Valley came Sullivan's American army, to burn the Indian towns and the Indian crops and to drive away the beaten Senecas and their British allies.

That raid of 1779 opened a rich, new land to settlement. Within a decade, many a Sullivan trooper, remembering the broad Valley where the grass grew so tall it hid a horse and rider from view, returned to the Genesee, over the old trails, not to the roll of the war drums but to the rumble of settlers' wagons.

> *"In the woodlands rang their axes,*
> *Smoked their towns in all the valleys."*

Most of the pioneers were men of humble birth and poor. But there also came to the Genesee late in the 18th Century two Wadsworth brothers from Connecticut, men of wealth and station.

They were the first of the landed gentry and they founded a land-holding dynasty and a tenant-farm, manor house, fox-hunting tradition that makes this Valley different from its neighbors. It is in the English pattern but it is utterly American. All these years squires, villagers and farmers have lived together in amity. There is no sharp class distinction in this Valley, no pulling of the forelock to the squires.

4

There was a time when the Valley was "The Breadbox of the Nation." For its wheat yield was the biggest and finest in all the land. A canal was dug and barges hauled the Genesee wheat to Rochester, to be ground in the gray stone mills beside the waterfalls. Blight and the plow that broke the Western plains combined to dim the luster of the wheat kingdom of the Genesee.

Some have, rather extravagantly, called this land "The Northern Bluegrass," because of the thoroughbred stock bred in the Valley for many years. Landed gentry and dirt farmers alike share a love of good horseflesh. The Genesee Valley Fox Hunt is the fourth oldest in America.

This is a many-sided land, a land of contrasts. The river that meanders so quietly through the rolling countryside has just tumbled over high waterfalls and coursed through a canyon so grand it defies description.

This Valley is so many things—the villages, some of them brisk trading centers, others drowsing away the years, all of them whispering of their New England heritage—the fields of golden wheat in the rolling land—the serene, winding river—17 miles of rock-walled gorge where thunder the falls of Portage—great estates with manor houses where fine stock crop the tall grass under oak trees—weatherbeaten farm houses out on the hills—a Fox Hunt and a Trappist monastery.

And there is the long cavalcade of history, lore and legend in which march Senecas, settlers, squires and Shakers—the Irish who dug the old canal—the fashionable folk lolling on the porches of the big wooden hotels when Avon Springs was a famous watering place—the gentle master of Glen Iris, a humanitarian who gave his estate with all its scenic gran-

5

deur to the people for a park—the deserted villages and ghost towns that are a part of the story of this Valley.

I have put some of these things between the pages of a book, a sort of sketch book of Valley events and Valley people.

To me, since I first heard it as a boy, the strangest, most compelling story of Valley time is that of Mary Jemison, the White Woman of the Genesee.

Chapter 2

The White Woman

The story begins on the sailing ship *William and Mary,* out of Londonderry, Ireland, and bound for Philadelphia. It is the Autumn of 1743.

While the ship is still at sea, Jane Erwin, wife of Thomas Jemison, gives birth to a baby girl. Her eyes are blue and they name her Mary.

The life that began amid the pounding of ocean waves against a sailing vessel ended 90 years later, in September of 1833, amid the wails of Indian mourners in the Seneca village on Buffalo Creek, where the industrial city of Buffalo roars today. Mary Jemison died as she lived ever since the Indians took her into captivity, a girl of 15—among the Indians.

Her story, one of the strangest on any frontier, will never die. It has become part of the folklore of America. The spirit of the White Woman will ever haunt her Valley of the Genesee.

She came there, long before the Revolution, the young bride of an Indian warrior, the first white woman to set foot in that lovely Valley.

There she lived for more than 70 years. There were years of peace and plenty mingled with years of war and trouble.

7

In the Valley she reared her seven half-breed children. There she buried her dead.

She saw the old Indian land invaded and her adopted people driven out. She clung to them when she might have rejoined her own people. She became the owner of many rich Valley acres. But her last years were full of trouble and she died virtually destitute.

She became a legend, the White Woman of the Genesee.

There is a bronze statue of the White Woman near the singing falls of Portage in the present Letchworth State Park. Thousands of tourists have seen it. It represents Mary as the young bride who walked from the Ohio to the Genesee, her papoose strapped upon her back, not as the bent old woman the first white settlers in the Valley knew.

Mary's story was written down in 1823 by James E. Seaver of Pembroke and put into a little book, which was published in 1824. Since then 23 editions of Seaver's "A Narrative of the Life of Mrs. Mary Jemison" have been issued. The book has been re-edited, abridged, illustrated and republished at 11 different places in the United States and Canada. The constant reprinting of the narrative proves its appeal through many generations.

The story of the Indian captive has been adapted for children's books. One wonders why Hollywood has overlooked it. People in far places who have only a vague idea where the Genesee Valley is have heard of the White Woman of the Genesee.

Yet here is a sample of conversation between two tourists— both from New York State—overheard at the Museum in Letchworth Park:

"Who is this Mary Jemison you hear so much about here?"

"Oh, she was an Indian princess."
In a sense she was.

*   *   *

When Mary came to tell her life story in her old age, she was not sure whether her parents were Scotch or Irish. It is probable her father was Scotch and her mother Irish. They were Protestants for the White Woman remembered the twice-daily devotions her father led in the family circle and the prayers her mother taught her.

She had two older brothers, John and Thomas Jr., and a sister, Betsey. Soon after landing in Philadelphia, the family took up land on the frontier, on Marsh Creek in Adams County, Pennsylvania. It is known today as the Buchanan Valley. There two more sons were born, Matthew and Robert.

The Jemison land was fertile and the family prospered in their new home set among the hills. Mary's dimming recollections of her girlhood were of a happy time. The child who was born on the ocean grew into a lovely girl, fair skinned with chestnut hair and deep blue eyes. She was slender and small of stature, hardly five feet tall, yet sturdy and never ill. There are tales in the Buchanan Valley of an early suitor although Mary was only 15 when the raiders came.

It was in April of 1758 and the breath of Spring was on the land. It was the time of the long French and Indian War and the Senecas were known to be on the warpath and not far away. But Thomas Jemison elected not to take his family to the stockade only six miles away. (Mary Jemison in her memoirs gave the year of her abduction as 1755. Research indicates that it was three years later.)

9

On the night of April 4, 1758, Mary was sent to a neighbor's house about a mile away to get a horse and return with it the next morning. On the way she had a strange vision—a white sheet seemed to descend and catch her up, saving her from a doom that threatened others. She always regarded it as an omen.

Returning home, she found her father shaving an axe helve in the yard, her mother busy preparing breakfast, her two older brothers in the barn. There are guests, a neighbor, his wife and their two children. The neighbor went to take care of the horse Mary had brought. Then a shot was heard, followed by the dreaded Indian war whoop. Six Indians and four Frenchmen ran out of the woods. They surrounded the house and took captive everyone save the two boys, unseen in the barn.

Prodded by whips, the prisoners are driven out into the woods. Along the way they see the body of the neighbor. That explains the shot. All day long the hapless settlers are marched over the rough trails without food or drink. At night they camp in the woods, carefully guarded.

At sunrise the Indians gave them some food after they had marched a while. Mary's mother kept up hope but her father was resigned to the worst.

After supper of the second day the Indians took off Mary's shoes and put moccasins on her feet. Her mother saw in that action an indication that the little girl would be spared.

Sixty-five years afterward, when the old White Woman of the Genesee was telling her story, tears rolled down her withered cheeks as she recalled her mother's parting words:

"Be careful and do not forget your English tongue . . . Don't try to escape for they will find and destroy you . . .

Don't forget the prayers I have taught you. I will always be with you. Be a good child and God will bless you."

The Indians took Mary and a boy captive away from the rest. That night around the fire, the Redskins began drying and scraping some scalps. Mary recognizes her mother's red hair. The girl, bred on the frontier, knows the fate of her family. But she hides her anguish and the Indians look at her approvingly. They are kind to this tiny, well-modeled girl with the fairest skin they had ever seen. To them she is a sort of goddess.

When Pennsylvania settlers in pursuit of the raiders found eight mutilated bodies, they concluded Mary was among the slain. For 40 years the captive was swallowed by the forest.

It was not until 1797 that the Rev. Timothy Alden, a missionary, learned from the mysterious White Woman who owned a vast tract along the Genesee that she was the Mary Jemison stolen by the Indians in that other valley so many years before.

*   *   *

Mary's life as an Indian really began at Fort Duquesne, the site of Pittsburgh, which was reached after a week's march through the forest. There were in the party, besides Mary and the little boy, a young man captive, 12 Indians and four Frenchmen.

At the fort, then in French and Indian hands, the Redskins painted the faces and hair of the prisoners crimson. In the morning the Frenchmen took the youth and the boy away. Mary never knew their fate. She was the only white left in the fort.

There she was given to two pleasant-faced Seneca sisters who had lost a brother in battle. They took her in a canoe

11

to an Indian village 80 miles down the Ohio River. Her foster mothers dressed Mary in new and clean Indian garb and threw her torn clothing into the river.

Mary Jemison never forgot the weird rites in which she was adopted by the Seneca women. The squaws of the village danced, tore their hair, gave vent to frenzied howls which culminated in cries of joy. Mary was now Dehgewanus. Her new Indian name meant "Two Falling Voices," symbolizing the end of the bereaved sisters' grief through the adoption of the white girl.

The sisters were gentle with Mary. She did only light chores around the cabin. The Senecas taught her their language but she kept repeating to herself English phrases and names and the prayers her mother had taught her. In this way she never allowed herself to forget her mother tongue. And always she kept her family name, Jemison.

After the British capture of Fort Duquesne, Mary was taken there with the Indians who made peace with the victors. But when English soldiers showed too much interest in the fair-haired captive, her alarmed foster mothers hurried her back to their home village.

After the sisters moved to a village on the Sciota, a group of Delawares joined them. It was decreed that Mary marry one of them, a tall young warrior named Sheninjee. She dared not disobey although the idea of marriage to an Indian was repugnant.

Her husband was brave, generous and kind. Their short married life was happy and Mary came to love him. Their first child, a girl, lived only two days. On the fourth winter on the Sciota, a son was born. Mary named him Thomas after her father—who had been slain by Indians.

Mary's Seneca sisters had gone to a tribal village on the

12

Genesee named Little Beard's Town (the present site of Cuylerville). They implored her to join them and Sheninjee consented to Mary's going. He planned to join them after the winter hunting.

So in the time of the ripened corn, Mary and her two Indian brothers set off on the long trek. The young mother, a nine-months old papoose strapped on her back, trudged some 600 miles, through an almost pathless wilderness, fording streams, sleeping on the ground in a wet blanket in the cold rains. Footsore, cold and sometimes hungry, she plodded on until she reached the Seneca stronghold on the Genesee where she received a warm welcome.

She was to remain in that fair valley of the natural clearings, beside the winding river, nearly all the rest of her long life.

Spring came but no Sheninjee. In Summer word comes that he is dead. He had sickened soon after the young couple parted on the Sciota.

For two years the young widow and her son lived in peace with the sisters. Then a crafty Dutch trader, John Van Sice, came to the village. He tried to kidnap the white girl, then in the full bloom of her blonde beauty, and take her to Fort Niagara where he would collect a bounty from the English under their system of ransoming white prisoners.

An Indian chief, in the trader's pay, was a party to the plot. But Mary and her baby hid for three days and three nights in an old cabin at Gardeau and in the tall weeds. The plotters gave up the attempt and left for Fort Niagara without her.

When Thomas was about four years old, Mary married again. Her new mate, Hiakatoo, was six feet tall and a famous and ferocious Seneca chief. He was over 60 and she

13

only 24 when they were married. For more than 40 years, until he died, she never wavered in her loyalty to the big Seneca.

With him she had security, for he was a powerful warrior, feared and respected by the Senecas. To them were born four daughters and two sons. Mary named the children after the white relatives she remembered—Jane, Betsy, Nancy, Polly, John and Jesse. Jane died at the age of 15.

Slowly the memories of her life in the green Pennsylvania Valley grew dim. She learns to count time by moons rather than months, to tell the seasons by the changing leaves and the ways of the animals. She has taken up the Indian way of life—and she never abandons it.

But it is significant that Mary gave all her children English names, indicating that she never forgot her white blood or considered herself an Indian. Thomas, the son of Sheninjee, and Jesse, the son of Hiakatoo, were fair and with blue eyes like their mother. They were of sunny disposition. John resembled his father, the warrior chief. No one would ever mistake him for a white man. And he was of quarrelsome nature.

While her boys were growing up, it was a happy time for Dehgewanus. The Revolution, called by the Indians "the Whirlwind," changed all that. Seaver quotes Mary as recalling:

"Thus at peace amongst ourselves and with the neighboring whites . . . our Indians lived quietly and peaceably at home until a little before the breaking out of the Revolutionary War."

The Indians were really pushed into that war. The rebellious colonists only wanted the Six Nations to remain neutral and at a conference at German Flats the chiefs

14

smoked the peace pipe and pledged themselves not to take part in the coming conflict.

But after a year the British called the same chiefs to a council in Oswego and asked their help in putting down the Revolution. The chiefs told of their agreement with the settlers. Finally the British won them over by telling them that the English king was rich and powerful, that the rebels were weak and would be easily subdued and that if the Indians would join the Redcoats, the tribes would never want for money, goods or favors.

So, Mary recalled, they came home laden with presents, each with a suit of clothes, a brass kettle, a tomahawk, a gun, a scalping knife, powder and lead, a gold piece and the promise of a bounty for every white scalp brought in to the British.

The British invited the Senecas to come to Fort Stanwix to watch the rebels take a whipping in battle. All the Indians had to do was to sit down, smoke their pipes and watch the fun. The Indians went but instead of being spectators, they had to fight for their lives. Thirty-six of them were killed and many wounded in the rout.

The peaceful days had gone from the Valley. Doleful wails for the dead in battle echoed through the village and the Senecas were full of vengeance and ready for the war path.

Hiakatoo became second in command of the Indian forces under the able Mohawk, Joseph Brant, and took part in the terrible massacre of settlers in the Wyoming Valley of Pennsylvania in 1778. The old chief was seldom at home with Mary and the children. Sometimes he would bring guests to stay overnight at the cabin, among them Brant and the notorious Col. John Butler, the Mohawk Valley Tory. Mary told of "washing their clothes and pounding samp all night for food for their journey."

There came a time when all the able-bodied males went to join their British allies in battle. The Seneca homeland was being invaded in the early Autumn of 1779 by an American army under Gen. John Sullivan.

After being beaten at Newtown on the Chemung, the Indians and British retreated, well ahead of the American army which was winding around the Finger Lakes and over the hills, burning every Seneca village on the way.

As "the Blue Snake," the Indians' name for Sullivan's army, writhed forward, there was consternation in Little Beard's Town, the Genesee Castle of the Senecas.

British and Indian forces ambushed a small American scouting party near the head of Conesus Lake and Mary told of the horrible tortures inflicted upon Lieut. Thomas Boyd and Sgt. Michael Parker, who were captured in the ambuscade.

A council of war decided against a fight at Genesee Castle. The warriors abandoned the village, hiding in the woods nearby. The old men, women and children were sent off toward Fort Niagara. Sullivan came and burned the deserted village and all the crops. It was his last stop in the campaign and "the Blue Snake" went back the way it had come.

Mary Jemison and three of her children were in the forlorn, fleeing party. One child she put on the back of her old horse, another she strapped to her back. The fugitives got at least as far as Varysburg in Wyoming County.

In late October, more than a month after Sullivan's departure, Mary and most of the Indian refugees returned to Genesee Castle. There they found only desolation.

Hiakatoo and Thomas were with the warriors. Mary and

her children had neither food nor shelter and winter was coming on. She thought of the cabin on Gardeau Flats where she had hidden from the Dutch trader. There she went with her children, one strapped on her back, the others following on foot.

Two runaway Negroes were living in the cabin. They had raised a large field of corn, which was ready for the harvest. They hired Mary to help them husk it. For pay she was to receive every tenth string. She wound up with 100 strings of ears or 25 bushels of shelled corn, enough to see her and her brood through the winter. The Negroes were kind to Mary. One of them kept his gun handy all the time she worked in the fields—as if Dehgewanus had anything to fear from Indians.

Mary and the children stayed with the Negroes all that winter, one of the most severe the White Woman ever knew. Five feet of snow covered the Valley and deer died of cold and hunger. So did some of the Senecas who had returned to the village.

The next season Mary made a shelter for herself at Gardeau. The Negroes went away the second year. Mary Jemison was to live on the Gardeau Flats for more than 50 years. She little dreamed in her time of trouble during the war that one day she would own virtually all those flats.

Mary saw the war parties leave the Genesee to raid frontier settlements and her heart was sad. But there was little she could do to stop such cruelty. The Indians were inflamed by a desire to avenge Sullivan's destruction of their homeland.

One such expedition into the Mohawk Valley was led by the great Seneca chief Cornplanter, the child of a forest romance between a dusky Indian maiden and a white trader

17

named John O'Bail. Mary revealed a hitherto unknown incident of that raiding campaign.

Cornplanter led his Indians to a cabin at Fort Plain. There two white prisoners were taken. Cornplanter, who had planned the raid, knew the older of the two captives but the old man with the white hair did not know the leader of the Indian band.

Fearfully the white man followed the chief to a secluded spot along the Mohawk. There they were alone and the younger man spoke in a kindly tone to his prisoner, who had expected to be tortured:

"My name is John O'Bail, commonly called Cornplanter. I am your son. You are my father. You are now my prisoner and subject to the customs of Indian warfare but you shall not be harmed.

"You need not fear. I am a warrior. Many are the scalps I have taken. Many prisoners have I tortured to death. I was anxious to see you and greet you in friendliness. I went to your cabin and took you by force. But your life shall be spared. Indians love their friends and their kindred and you shall be treated with kindness.

"If now you choose to follow the fortunes of your yellow son and live with our people, I will cherish your old age with plenty of venison and you shall live easy, but if it is your choice to return to your fields and to live with your white children, I will send a party of my young men to conduct you in safety. I respect you, my father. You have been friendly to Indians and they are your friends."

John O'Bail chose to return to his white children and Cornplanter, the son whom he had not recognized, provided the escort just as he had promised.

About 1782 Ebenezer "Indian" Allen, who later was to

be the first white settler on the site of Rochester, struck up a friendship with Thomas Jemison and stayed at Mary's cabin for a time. He was in trouble with the British and was hiding from them. Allen had a reputation for violence and cruelty. He had been an officer in the British army. He also was a polygamist and one of his wives was an Indian.

Mary was to meet "Indian" Allen again—in 1792 when he ran a saw mill at the Silver Lake Outlet near the river and the White Woman carried on her back the boards for her daughter's house at Gardeau which had been sawed at the Allen mill some five miles away.

Mary said that Allen "was always honorable, kind and even generous with me" but she added, according to Seaver, that "the history of his life is a tissue of crimes and baseness of the blackest dye." She said that Allen delighted in relating "his infamous crimes."

After the Revolution, Hiakatoo came back to Mary and the children at Gardeau. He was greatly aged and no longer in robust health. The warpath had taken its toll.

Shortly Mary was called upon to make a momentous decision. Her Seneca brother came to her, offering her the opportunity to rejoin the white people if she so desired.

Thomas urged her to go and offered to accompany her. But the chiefs of the tribe decreed that the fair-skinned son of Sheninjee could not be spared. He showed too much promise as a warrior and a counselor. Mary had come to rely greatly on her oldest son and she decided to stay with the Indians. She also feared that her Indian children would not be warmly received by her white kin and she was resolved to keep the family together. Besides the old chief needed her—and she had lived the Indian way so long.

Pleased at her decision, the Seneca brother told her he

would see that she would have a tract on which she could live and pass on to her children. He went to Canada where he died. Ten years went by before Mary heard any more about her land.

In the late Summer of 1797 a great council of whites and Indians convened on the banks of the Genesee at Big Tree near the present Geneseo. The council was called to arrange for the Seneca Nation's relinquishing more than three and one half million acres of land west of the Genesee to Robert Morris, the land speculator.

Farmer's Brother, an influential Seneca chief, called Mary to the council. He said her Indian brother had spoken to him long ago about reserving a tract for Dehgewanus and that now was the time to select her land.

Mary named the bounds of the tract she desired. She shrewdly told Thomas Morris of Canandaigua, representing his father at the treaty fire, that she has tilled patches here and there and wanted an extension of her tract. Morris little knew the extent of her demand.

Lockwood L. Doty wrote in his *History of Livingston County* a half century later that "At the Treaty of Big Tree Mary Jemison took part in the deliberations both in and out of the council house, urging her claims for an allotment of land in a manner that was more pertinacious than dignified."

The White Woman who had known so much adversity was fighting for a big prize—security for herself and her children. Farmer's Brother presented her claim earnestly. Red Jacket, the orator of the Nation, spoke in opposition with fire and eloquence. Red Jacket kicked up considerable fuss at Big Tree. At one time he angrily extinguished the treaty fire although he had no right to do so. The orator was in his cups when Farmer's Brother pushed through Mary's claim.

It was a grand prize Mary had won—the Gardeau Reservation of 17,297 acres, six miles wide and four and three quarters miles long on both sides of the Genesee. It was fertile land and it became known on the frontier as "The White Woman's Tract." Today much of it is a part of Letchworth State Park.

Red Jacket not only opposed the White Woman's claim at the council but for two years he withheld from her money which belonged to her, because the land had been granted without his consent. Horatio Jones, and Jasper Parrish, white interpreters, finally made the orator turn over the money.

The White Woman received permission from the government to lease a large part of her land to white farmers on shares. Now she was a landed proprietor with a tenant system—like the aristocratic Wadsworths of Big Tree.

Her holdings included 300 acres of unforested land. The Indians believed this tract had been cleared by some prehistoric race and Mary seems to have shared their belief.

Major events in the Valley during Mary's early occupancy of her reservation were the death of Little Beard, the chief for whom a town was named, and the eclipse of the sun a few days after his funeral.

That generation of Indians had never seen a total eclipse of the sun and the daytime darkness terrified them. They gathered, beating their drums and chanting. Believing that the spirit of Little Beard, on its way up the heavenly path, had obscured the sun, they shot their arrows and bullets skyward until the brightness was restored.

Despite her many acres, the White Woman in her late

years was far from happy. Peace and quiet did not last long at Gardeau. Mary's greatest joy was in her children. All seven were living, except Jane who died at the age of 15 the year of the Big Tree Treaty. Mary saw that each had a home on her reservation. With her own hands she built a cabin on the flats for Nancy.

Thomas was the apple of his mother's eye. She gave him the prized Squawkie Hill farm, near an old Indian reservation celebrated in tribal history. Thomas was a kind, wise and gentle man except when he was in his cups. Then he was quarrelsome and unmanageable.

In her old age Mary Jemison bitterly deplored the effect of the white man's firewater on the Indian character. She regarded liquor as the great curse of her adopted people.

From early boyhood there had been hostility between the light complected Thomas and the swarthy John. The pair had many arguments but never fought except when Thomas was drinking. Then he was a wild man. Once he struck the aged Hiakatoo and even raised a tomahawk over his mother's head.

It was on July 1, 1811 that the first tragedy struck. That day 49-year-old Thomas came to his mother's home. Mary was away but John was home. The half brothers began drinking and quarreling.

Mary returned home, to find her son dead by the door. John had grabbed Thomas by the hair, dragged him out the door and killed him with a blow from his tomahawk. He said Thomas had upbraided him for having two wives and had started the quarrel.

Sick with sorrow, Mary sent a messenger to Buffalo Creek to inform the chiefs of the murder and to ask a council to

22

The White Woman in Youth and in Her Old Age

Mary Jemison Statue and Log Cabin in Letchworth Park

determine John's punishment. The slayer in the meantime fled toward Caneadea.

The council exonerated him on the ground that Thomas had been the aggressor. John was Hiakatoo's favorite son and the old chief still was a power among his people. Ordinarily killing of a brother was a cardinal sin in the Indian code and would merit death. John came back to Gardeau but some people shunned him. Among them was his own brother, Jesse, who tried to take the dead Thomas' place as his mother's protector and standby.

That November Hiakatoo breathed his last. He was, as near as could be reckoned, 103 years old. For four years he had been dying of consumption. He had been a mighty and a ruthless warrior. Mary never condoned his cruelty to enemies but also remembered his tenderness toward his friends and his uniform kindness to her during the fifty years they lived together.

And she paid this tribute to his virility: "He was an old man when I first saw him but he was no means enervated."

The old warrior was buried in Mary's private graveyard on the Reservation, in the Indian fashion, in his best raiment and with his war implements, his tomahawk, war club, hunting knife, powder flask and flint, along with a cake and a cup.

In May of the next year, 1812, the widowed White Woman again knew a great sorrow. Another son was murdered by a brother—after another drinking bout.

It came about when her sons, John and Jesse, and her son-in-law, George Shongo, were helping Robert Whaley, a Castile pioneer, and other workers in his pay slide boards from the top of a hill to the river above the Lower Falls. Whaley had built a raft to take the boards to market down river.

23

Before the trio left Gardeau, Mary implored them not to do any drinking. Her plea was ignored. They drank and toward nightfall Shongo and Jesse had a fight in which Shongo was worsted.

Then after Whaley and most of the other workmen had left, Jesse aroused from a stupor to confront John who had a knife in his hand. They exchanged hot words and Jesse tried to seize the knife. They struggled and fell together. John, beneath his brother, stabbed Jesse repeatedly until finally the younger brother cried out: "Brother, you have killed me."

His body bore 18 stab wounds, any one of which would have caused death. Mary was frantic with grief when his mangled body was brought to her cabin. She lamented: "My darling son, him on whom I depended is dead and I in my old age am left destitute of a helping hand."

Jesse was buried in Mary's cemetery "after the manner of burying white people." He was only about 28, had his mother's sunny nature and was inclined to copy the whites in manners and dress. He shunned the company of Indians generally and this probably led to John's hatred of him.

Again a bereaved mother raised her voice to denounce the sale of firewater to Indians. She knew had her Jesse been sober, he would have avoided the fight with the surly John.

Mary also knew disillusionment and was the prey of an imposter. Around 1810 a man turned up at Gardeau, claiming he was George Jemison, her cousin. He said he was the son of her father's brother. The White Woman had never heard of her father having any brother other than one who was killed at Fort Necessity in the French and Indian war.

But with characteristic generosity she gave this man and his family a place to live on her reservation, bought him a cow, paid his debts and in every way treated him as a kinsman.

Her kindness was rewarded by the imposter's trying to defraud her of a large tract of land. When she sent a grandson, one of Thomas' sons, to get back her cow from the spurious relative, Jemison clubbed the boy and sought to have him arrested. Mary, at last convinced the man was no kin of hers, got him off her land.

Her son John, slayer of two brothers, led a turbulent life. He had some skill with herbs and roots and was known among the Indians as a medicine man. He was continually drinking and fighting. During a carousal with two Squawkie Hill Indians, a quarrel arose. One of the Indians dragged John off his horse and struck him on the head with a rock. John tried to get to a nearby hut but the Indians fell on him, cut his throat and brained him with an axe. That was on June 30, 1817 and John was 54 years old.

Again the White Woman buried a son "in the manner of the white people" in the little cemetery—beside the two brothers he had slain. John had never been her favorite. He had never given her anything but trouble.

*   *   *

The story of Mary Jemison's generosity to a needy stranger who came to her door has survived nearly 150 years. It was in 1806, a year when drought killed virtually all the crops in the Genesee Country.

Truman Stone, a pioneer of Orangeville, set out on horseback in search of grain and corn he desperately needed to keep his family alive. He traveled far up and down the trails but everywhere the fields were barren. No one had enough food for his own use, to say nothing of having any to sell at any price.

Finally Stone came to the White Woman's cabin. He offered $5 for a bushel of corn. Mary replied that she "would not sell him a bushel of corn for a bushel of dollars."

She asked Stone when he had eaten last. When he told it was breakfast the day before, Mary invited him in, swung a kettle over the fire and made an Indian cake of salted cracked corn. She added a goose egg to the dish and while Stone was eating, she went up to her attic and returned with a pillowcase full of shelled corn from her scanty store. When the stranger offered to pay for it, the White Woman said with quiet dignity: "No, I will take no pay. Take this to your family."

On his way home, Stone found a thin fringe of wheat ripening in his field. He reaped a few bundles, dried them around the fire, threshed them and had them ground in the mill at Varysburg. That night his family supped on short cake and butter, their first square meal in weeks. With the bit of wheat and Mary's corn they beat the famine that drab year of 1806.

That was the story Truman Stone told at the festive board every Thanksgiving as long as he lived—how the "pagan" White Woman gave up without hesitation what money could not buy in a time of famine.

Mary saw many changes in her Valley. In May of 1817 a large chunk of the heavily timbered High Banks gave way with a mighty crash and slid into the Genesee, forcing the river into a new channel to the east. The Great Slide was only about 200 yards south of Mary's stout timbered house with the shingled roof and her well-filled frame barn.

There were changes other than the course of the river.

More and more white settlers were moving into the region. The forests were being cut down. The Indians were leaving. Mary had considerable influence with those who remained and often was an intermediary between them and the white settlers.

The white newcomers regarded with curiosity the little bent old woman who had twice been married to an Indian and who owned so much land. At first Mary was shy and reserved with her new neighbors but she thawed out as she got to know them.

When they were ill, she brewed tea for them, made from herbs she had collected. She showed them where the choicest wild berries grew. She was a familiar figure on the roads and in the settlements. Often she was carrying some heavy burden, Indian fashion, with the load suspended across her back with a strap which passed across her forehead. White children who went to her cabin found her kindly and smiling. Generally they came away with gifts from the White Woman.

For years white men had been casting longing eyes at Mary's many acres. It was good land but the White Woman, her family and tenants could not work the whole acreage and some of it had grown up to weeds. That fact, along with her age and the influx of whites, impelled the White Woman to consider sale of her reservation.

As early as 1816 Jellis Clute and Micah Brooks, men of consequence in the region, began negotiations for purchase of part of Mary's land. It was seven years before the deal was finally closed. A special act of the Legislature had to be passed before Mary could legally transfer her title. Also the approval of the Seneca Nation and the United States gov-

27

ernment had to be obtained. Henry B. Gibson of Canandaigua joined Brooks and Clute in the purchase.

Mary was to receive an annuity of $300 during her lifetime, the sum to be paid annually after her death to "her heirs and assigns forever." She reserved for herself a tract of two square miles and a smaller parcel for her friend and benefactor, Thomas Clute. The part she retained was known as the White Woman's Reserve.

The sale of the Gardeau flats opened a large new tract to white settlement and the purchasers lost no time in offering lots for sale to settlers.

It was shortly after she sold her land that Mary Jemison was induced to tell her strange story for publication. Daniel Bannister, publisher, engaged Dr. James E. Seaver to write the old woman's memoirs.

The White Woman met Bannister and Seaver at the home of Mrs. Jennet Whaley in the Town of Castile and stayed there three days telling her life story. She walked the four miles from her home at Gardeau "without a staff," Seaver noted, although she was then 80 years of age.

The years had faded the eyes of Irish blue and dimmed their sight somewhat. The chestnut hair, tied in a knob behind her head, had turned gray but it still was curly. But despite all her years of outdoor life, she had retained the pink and white complexion of her girlhood.

Seaver reported that she walked with a quick step, her head carried forward because she had carried so many loads on her back with a strap across her forehead.

She spoke clearly and her English was mixed with Irish idiom. Sometimes, as she unfolded her story, tears rolled down her cheeks. Her remarkable memory, especially for names and dates, excited Seaver's admiration.

The White Woman told her biographer that she has always worked hard and still did. She pounded her samp, cooked her meals, chopped her wood, fed her cattle, tended her garden and sometimes helped in the fields.

Unaccustomed to chairs, she sat on the floor or a bench. Her bed was a mound of skins on the floor and she held her victuals in her lap or in her hand as she ate. She had lived the Indian way for 65 years.

Her garb was Indian and to white people's eyes outlandish. Her ensemble consisted of a brown flannel short gown with long sleeves, the shirt reaching to her hips and tied in two places with doeskin strings. A blue cloth skirt was tied about her waist and reached to the calves of her legs, which were encased in blue cloth leggings. Buckskin moccasins clad her feet, along with some rags which served as stockings. It was Autumn and coolish and Mary wore a blanket over her shoulders and an ancient brown woolen bonnet on her head.

James Seaver wrote down the White Woman's story for posterity—unfortunately not in her own words but in his own sometimes stilted style. Publication of the book aroused wide interest and the frontier girl, who as a captive of the Indians became Dehgewanus and as a land owner was known as The White Woman, in her old age became a figure of history.

And today there are many who are proud to boast that "my great-grandmother knew Mary Jemison." Some of those pioneer ancestors had looked askance at the old lady in her Indian garb and sniffed at her record of marriage to two Indians, with the resultant brood of half-breeds.

In 1825 the Senecas had sold all their reservations along the Genesee and moved to the Tonawanda, Cattaraugus and Buffalo Creek reserves.

29

Mary, her daughters and their husbands on the Gardeau Flats, feeling themselves hemmed in by whites, determined to move to "Indian country." So in 1831 the White Woman sold her remaining two square miles, traded her annuity for ready cash and moved to the Buffalo Creek reservation. There she bought a farm at what was known as "Frog Pond," on the bank of Buffalo Creek and near the present Jemison Road in the city of Buffalo.

During her many years with the Indians, the White Woman had adhered to the faith of her adopted people while never forgetting the prayers her mother had taught her in the Pennsylvania valley.

When a white missionary sought to convert her to Christianity in her last years by telling her she must "repent of her sins" to be "saved," she retorted:

"Saved, saved; what mean ye? I have tried to live good; I have not sinned against your God or the Great White Spirit. I have been dragged almost to your hell and I have been tempted; but my good mother has always been with me as she promised. Saved! I am not afraid to die, if that is what ye mean."

At Buffalo Creek she came under the influence of more tactful missionaries, the Rev. Asher Wright and his wife. She went to the Indian Mission school they conducted on Buffam Street. And in the Summer of 1833 she formally joined the Christian faith. It was almost a deathbed conversion for on Sept. 19, 1833, Mary Jemison breathed her last. She was 90 years old.

She was given a Christian burial in the Indian cemetery on the reservation and her funeral was well attended. A marble slab inscribed "In Memory of the White Woman," marked her grave.

Her three surviving children, Betsey, Nancy and Polly, all died within three months in the Fall of 1839. Two grandsons, children of Thomas Jemison, became successful and respected citizens.

One of them, Thomas, called "Buffalo Tom," in 1818 built a log house which still stands on Squawkie Hill, south of Mount Morris. Two clapboard wings have been added to it and tarpaper covers the logs, put together with wooden plugs and mortar. There is a plaque on its side and a historical marker in front of the old house. Similarly marked is the spring nearby the White Woman was wont to visit.

"Buffalo Tom" moved to Buffalo Creek in 1828 where he kept a tavern. Later he had a large farm on the Cattaraugus Reservation along the Cattaraugus Creek. There he died in 1887.

A leader in the councils of the Seneca Nation for many years, he was one of the Indian delegates to a conference on Indian affairs in Washington called by President Andrew Jackson. Jackson gave Jemison a large silver medal for his services and the grandson of the White Woman always wore it around his neck at public gatherings.

His brother, Jacob, attended Dartmouth College and practiced medicine. He became an assistant surgeon in the United States Navy and was highly regarded by his superiors.

About Jacob clings a romantic tale which is probably apocryphal. He was aboard the cruiser *Powhatan* which was sent to the Mediterranean in pursuit of pirates. The ship docked at Algiers. There he met the daughter of a local sheik. It was love at first sight but marriage was impossible. And shortly the *Powhatan* had its sailing orders. Jacob had to leave his beautiful Fatima.

When the cruiser arrived at Cyprus, she was found aboard,

31

a stowaway. The lovers had to part again. The girl was sent back to her father. Several years later Jacob died aboard his ship and was buried at sea. What became of the lovely Algerian is not recorded. Probably she married a sheik and mothered many dark-skinned children.

For four decades the bones of Mary Jemison rested in the burying ground at Buffalo Creek while a city grew up around the old Indian reservation.

In 1859 a wealthy and public spirited industrialist, William Pryor Letchworth, had established an estate in the scenic wonderland of waterfalls and canyon that is now Letchworth State Park. He called his home Glen Iris.

Letchworth became deeply interested in the history and Indian lore of the Genesee Country. In 1870 he had at his own expense moved the old Seneca Council House from Caneadea to Glen Iris.

The fantastic story of Mary Jemison fascinated him and in 1874 he had her remains brought from Buffalo to be reinterred near the Council House, where so long ago she had stopped on her long trek from the Ohio to the Genesee.

George Shongo, a grandson of the White Woman, brought Mary back to her Valley. In the center of her grave at Buffalo Creek he had found an oddly-shaped porcelain dish which probably had contained food when it was placed there. In it was the remains of a wooden spoon. Mary Jemison may have had a Christian burial but the "pagan" Indians had added their own touch according to their ancient customs.

"Buffalo Tom" Jemison planted a black walnut tree at his grandmother's grave. It is still there. Letchworth had the grave curbed from stones from the Indian cemetery at Gardeau. White settlers had plowed them up and used them for a culvert until the master of Glen Iris rescued them.

Letchworth envisioned a heroic bronze statue of the White Woman atop the plain stone which was placed on her grave in 1874. He commissioned sculptor Henry K. Bush-Brown to fashion a life-size statue of Mary Jemison, not as the tired old woman the first white settlers knew, but as the young bride who had come on foot to the Genesee so long ago, her babe strapped upon her back. The wise old man saw to it that the artist caught the lithe grace and comeliness of the White Woman in the bloom of her youth. The statue was dedicated Sept. 19, 1910, the 77th anniversary of Mary Jemison's death.

Letchworth also brought from Gardeau the log house that Mary had built for her daughter, Nancy.

So today there is a little corner of the state park that is dedicated to Mary Jemison and the Senecas with whom she lived so long. Thousands visit the Council House, the statue and the log cabin.

The White Woman is not forgotten in her own country. Annually the Castile Historical Society presents in Letchworth Park a historical pageant built upon Mary's life.

No frontier girl was ever forced to lead a stranger life. Mary Jemison's years were full of toil and woe. Yet she never lost her sunny smile, her fortitude or her abiding generosity.

Chapter 3

The Ambuscade

By the flickering light of candles, four generals in the buff and blue of the American Revolutionary army pored over their maps in a tent in the hills of the Genesee Country on the night of Sept. 12, 1779.

Their army had encamped for the night at what is now Foot's Corners east of Conesus Lake. They had hoped to make the Indian town at the head of the lake but night had set in too soon.

The four officers met in the tent of their leader, Maj. Gen. John Sullivan of New Hampshire. The others, all brigadiers, were Enoch Poor of New Hampshire, William Maxwell of New Jersey and Edward Hand of Pennsylvania. All were seasoned veterans.

John Sullivan, tenacious, outspoken and courageous, had been selected by George Washington to lead this expedition of some 4,000 men into the Seneca country in retaliation for British-Indian raids on border settlements and to stop the flow of supplies to the Redcoats.

He was 39 years old and he had come a long way up from chore boy in Portsmouth. A lawyer and a member of the first Continental Congress, he was one of Washington's most trusted lieutenants. He had served in Eastern campaigns and most of them had been losing ones, for the Americans were always outnumbered and ill equipped.

But this campaign had been a success. True his men were tired and often they were hungry. They had had to cut their way through a wilderness. Still all the way from Tioga Point (Athens), Pa., where they had been joined by Maj. Gen. James Clinton's New York Brigade, their path had been a victorious one.

At Newtown in the Chemung Valley the British-Indian allies had made their stand and had been decisively beaten. After that Sullivan never came to grips with the enemy, in full retreat. The Americans marched over the hills around the lovely Finger Lakes sparkling in the summer sunshine, burning every Seneca village, destroying all the standing crops and ruining the orchards along the way. Another American general, named Sherman, was to blaze a similar path of desolation "from Atlanta to the sea" 85 years later.

Now the expedition was in the Genesee Country and near the end of its campaign. One stronghold of the Senecas remained to be reduced. That was the Genesee Castle of Chief Little Beard, near the present Cuylerville.

But Sullivan found that his maps and the information of Indian guides as to the exact location of this important town disagreed. It turned out the Indians were right.

The conference ended at 11 o'clock with Sullivan deciding upon sending a scouting party to find the Castle and report back at once.

To lead this party he picked Lieut. Thomas Boyd of the celebrated Morgan Riflemen, now led by Major James Parr. The 22-year-old Pennsylvanian, handsome, vital, enthusiastic, came to his commander's tent.

What transpired there is a matter of dispute. Some historians claim Sullivan told Boyd to take only four men along. Others contend that the size of the party was left to Boyd's discretion.

In his official report, a month later, the commander gave this version:

"I had the preceding evening ordered out an officer with three or four riflemen, one of our guides and an Oneida chief to reconnoitre the Chinesee town that we might, if possible, surprise it. Lieutenant Boid (sic) was the officer entrusted with the service, who took with him 23 men, volunteers from the same corps and a few from Colonel Butler's regiment, making in all 26, a much larger number than I had thought of sending and by no means so likely to answer the purpose. . . ."

Boyd was only 22 years old but he was a veteran of four years service in some of the toughest campaigns of the war. It seems hardly likely that he would deliberately disobey his commanding officer.

Of Scottish descent, Thomas Boyd was a native of Northumberland, Pa. His father died young, leaving three sons and a daughter. The widow Boyd saw her three boys go off to war and none of them returned. The eldest, John, was captured by Indians and was never seen again. William fell at the battle of Brandywine in 1777.

Thomas, the youngest, as a mere boy of 18 was with Benedict Arnold's troops in the ill-starred expedition against Quebec in '75. He was wounded, discharged and returned to Pennsylvania. He re-enlisted in the first Pennsylvania and was at the battle of Saratoga. He heard the turkey gobble war cry of Dan Morgan's riflemen in the woods, little thinking he one day was to be an officer in the celebrated Morgan Rifle Corps, although the big Virginian no longer was to command it. He saw Gentleman Johnny Burgoyne's scarlet-clad army lay down its arms at Saratoga in '77.

Promoted to lieutenant, he served with Washington's army and was at Monmouth where the usually imperturbable commander-in-chief roundly cursed Gen. Charles Lee for his inexcusable retreat.

In 1778 Boyd was sent with a detachment of Morgan Riflemen to Schoharie to protect that border settlement against enemy raids.

Thomas Boyd would like to forget Schoharie. It was there he had met that village belle, Cornelia. She had fallen in love with the handsome lieutenant and then she was with child, just as orders came for Boyd's company to join Clinton's army, massing at Otsego Lake for the expedition against the Senecas.

Cornelia had come to the camp while Boyd's men were waiting for his order to move. She had flung herself upon the lieutenant, had tearfully implored him to marry her before he left Schoharie. He had tried to calm her by evasive promises and then she had solemnly declared that if he would not marry her, she hoped and prayed he would be "cut up and tortured by the savages."

Then came the supreme mortification of having his commander, Colonel Butler, ride up and reprimand him for keeping his troops waiting. No, Tom Boyd did not like to think of Schoharie and how he had thrust the tearful girl aside before he marched away. He never saw the belle of Schoharie again. Nor did he ever see the daughter that was born later that Fall—after he had met the savages.

Such is the story that has been handed down through the years although some historians have disputed its accuracy.

The Oneida chief who went with Boyd was Hanyerry, a

Picture by Katherine Merrill

Remains of Old Valley Canal near Nunda

When the Canal Wound above River Gorge

skilled guide. Also in the detachment was the fabulous Timothy Murphy of Pennsylvania, he of the 32 Indian scalps and the fearsome gun with the two barrels that so baffled the Redskins.

Before daybreak the party came upon the deserted Indian village near the present Hampton Corners. Boyd and Murphy stole ahead of the others and spotted four Indians. The trigger-happy Timothy fired, killing one. The rest fled. Tim collected his 33d scalp. Boyd sensed the danger. Those Indians would spread the alarm. He resolved to rejoin the main army and sent two runners back to Sullivan, telling of the incident.

As the scouts picked their way toward the head of Conesus Lake, Boyd sent two more messengers ahead to warn the main army. They came back with a report there were five Indians ahead. Boyd's patrol chased them but they kept just out of reach. The lieutenant knew then that the Senecas had support in the neighborhood and quickened the march back to Sullivan's base.

They were on Groveland Hill, only a mile from safety and they could hear the beat of Hand's drums in the valley below, when suddenly the awful Seneca war whoop sounded. Out of a ravine where they had hidden sprang 600 Indians and British under the Mohawk chief, Joseph Brant, and Walter Butler, the notorious Ranger.

These remnants of the allied army beaten at Newtown, plus reinforcements from Fort Niagara, were lurking in the hills, waiting for a chance to attack the main American force. Possibly Boyd's ill-fated little expedition, stumbling on the enemy, saved Sullivan's army, which would have to pass the place of ambuscade on its way to Genesee Castle.

Courageously, Boyd tried to break out of the trap. At first

39

his fire told heavily on the foe. Three times the Americans charged. But the odds were hopeless—600 to 22. Sixteen died on the spot. The Oneida, Hanyerry, was one of them. Boyd and Sgt. Michael Parker of the Pennsylvania troops were taken prisoner. Four, including Tim Murphy who tumbled a big warrior in his dash, escaped.

Meanwhile the base uneasily awaited news of the scouting party. Survivors came racing into camp with word of the ambuscade. The light troops were rushed to the scene of massacre. The enemy had vanished, leaving behind a wagon load of packs and other provisions, a dead Indian—and the slain Americans. There was no sign of Thomas Boyd or Michael Parker. The soldiers buried their dead in two graves on a little hill overlooking the ravine of ambuscade.

On Sept. 14, the whole American army marched in regular order across the Genesee flats and forded the river. The grass in the river bottoms was so tall that sometimes only the guns of the soldiers were visible above the waving brown mass.

Sullivan found an empty Genesee Castle. The Indians, men, women and children, Mary Jemison among them, had left for Fort Niagara, escorted by Butler's troops. Fires were still fresh in some of the 128 well-built Seneca houses. Great heaps of corn the Indian women had gathered lay on the ground. Sullivan's troops burned the houses and all the crops. Little Beard's proud castle was only smoldering ashes.

At dusk Paul Sanborn, a soldier of the Clinton Brigade, found the horribly mutilated and headless corpse of young Thomas Boyd and nearby in the long grass the body of Michael Parker. Both had been fiendishly tortured.

The prisoners had been brought to Genesee Castle and interviewed by Brant and Butler, who tried to find out Sulli-

40

van's strength and plans. Exactly what happened is veiled in legend and mystery. There is a tale that Boyd gave his fellow Mason, Brant, the fellowship's signal of distress and that Brant responded. But, so the story goes, Brant found it expedient to be elsewhere when the two Americans were turned over to the red warriors for exquisite torture.

Certainly their deaths had been horrible. Their comrades buried the two Pennsylvanians, the lieutenant and the sergeant, under the wild plum trees, near the junction of two creeks, known thereafter as Boyd and Parker Creeks.

And one wonders if Cornelia, back in Schoharie and soon to bear a child, remembered the curse of "torture by the savages" she had put on her recreant lover a few weeks before.

Genesee Castle was the last stand of Sullivan's army. The general declared "mission accomplished" and the troops marched back the way they had come. Many of them would be coming back again within a decade, not as warriors but as settlers in the old Indian land they had despoiled. The Sullivan-Clinton expedition blazed a trail of white settlement, as well as a path of Seneca ruin.

For 72 years the bones of Boyd and Parker remained at "the Torture Tree" near Cuylerville and those of their comrades where they had fallen in ambuscade on Groveland Hill.

In 1841 the City of Rochester induced Livingston County to part with the remains of the martyrs and they were reinterred in Mount Hope Cemetery's Revolutionary Hill. A wooden box containing the bones of the Revolutionary veterans was brought by canal boat from the Valley and there were military parades, oratory and much ceremony.

Governor Seward and other notables were on the speakers' stand at Mount Hope. Paul Sanborn, now 79 and an old

41

settler at Conesus, was there. He was the one who first found the Boyd and Parker bodies in the long grass at Little Beard's Town in 1779.

A sudden downpour halted the ceremonies and scattered the crowd. There is a story old men tell that the wooden sarcophagus was never buried in Mount Hope because of the storm and that some boys, poking around in the cemetery later, found it and scattered its contents to the winds.

In a few years Rochester voted to abandon Revolutionary Hill. It was leveled off and made into a private burial place. The remains of Boyd, Parker and the others were consigned to Potter's Field, that last abode of the poor and friendless. Rochester did not cover itself with glory as custodians of the remains of the Revolutionary heroes.

In 1879, the centennial of the Sullivan campaign, the bones of the martyrs were rescued from the ignominy of Potter's Field, largely through the efforts of Rochester's Irondequoit Chapter, Daughters of the American Revolution. The remains were moved to Patriot Hill, a soldiers' burial plot. In 1903 an inscribed boulder was placed at the graves and every Memorial Day special services are held there.

There's a little park with a boulder, a wayside shrine, at the site of "the Torture Tree," east of Cuylerville, honoring Thomas Boyd and Michael Parker. On Sept. 14, 1929, the 150th anniversary of the occupation of Genesee Castle, a dedication ceremony and elaborate pageant drew thousands to the scene.

And on a little hill overlooking the ravine where Butler and Brant hid in ambush in 1779 is a plain white shaft behind an iron fence. It was put there in 1901 by the Livingston County Historical Society. It marks "the scene of the massacre after a desperate and heroic struggle of Lt. Boyd's scouting party of Gen. Sullivan's army by an ambuscade of British and Indians under Butler and Brant Sept. 13, 1779."

There are other names graven on the monument, the names of "Hanyerry, a loyal Oneida chief; Sgt. Nicholas Hungerman and Privates John Carney, William Faughey, John McElroy, John Miller, Benjamin Curtin, John Putnam and several others, names unknown, who fell and were buried here."

They fell far from their homes, these men, some with old English names, others smacking of Irish, Scotch and German extraction and one member of the race that ruled the land before the palefaces came. The monument on the hillock not only marks the site of the only engagement of the Revolution in the Genesee Valley—and it was a minor engagement at that. It also is a shrine to the patriots of old, the citizen soldiers who dared the might of Britain that a country might be free. It was acquired by the state in 1935.

Until this Autumn of 1955 the shrine was hard to get to. The monument is back in the fields off the Gray Road and there was no path. As this is written, the Town of Groveland is building a road to the scene, along with a parking area, to make the historic site more accessible.

It is the most peaceful, sylvan spot imaginable when you get there and it is hard to realize that once it heard the savage war whoop, the whizz of flying arrows, the rattle of musketry and the screams of dying men.

Chapter 4

"Davy Crocketts"

The current idol of young America is a fabulous frontiersman from the hills of Tennessee named Davy Crockett. Possibly you've heard a song about him.

In the olden time there were fabulous frontiersmen in the Valley of the Genesee, too. But nobody wrote songs about them, although Genesee fits as neatly into rhyme as Tennessee.

Particularly there were two "kings of the wild (Genesee) frontier" whose adventures and exploits make the life of Davy Crockett seem that of a mild, sedentary semi-invalid.

They shot b'ar and Injuns and they wore coonskin caps. They were seasoned woodsmen, scouts, soldiers before Davy Crockett was born.

Like the hero of Kipling's poem, they were wont "to jest at the dawn with death." They bore charmed lives. Both lived to a good old age and died in their beds.

There was no crack in the Liberty Bell in their time. For they were soldiers of the Revolution.

Their names were Horatio Jones and Moses Van Campen.

*   *   *

Horatio Jones was born in Downingtown, Chester County, Pa., in 1763 of Welsh ancestry. His father was a gunsmith

45

and the boy learned enough of that trade to stand him in good stead in after years.

The curly-haired, fair-skinned, cool-eyed, sinewy lad grew up on the frontier with no formal schooling. But he had a quick mind and he was well trained in marksmanship, running, horsemanship, woods lore and rough and tumble wrestling. And he could play the fife.

He was only 13 when he ran away from home to join a company of Minute Men of the Revolution. He joined up as a fifer but he could shoot straight, too.

At the age of 16 he enlisted in the Bedford Rangers and was a member of a scouting party that was ambushed by a band of Indians and British along the Juanita River one June day in 1781. Nine Americans were killed and eight were taken prisoner. Among the captives was young Horatio Jones.

The first days of his long captivity were not soon to be forgotten. Each prisoner was hobbled by a blanket tied about his thighs so he could not run away. For two days the prisoners were driven along the trail like cattle. On the third day Jones was given the entrails of a bear for his supper.

On the fourth day when the Indians mistakenly thought Horatio was trying to escape, they seized him, laid him on his back, tied his arms and legs, drove pronged sticks into his body and left him there all night, with the rain falling on his upturned face.

When the Indians saw that the youth "could take it," they treated him more kindly, especially after they saw him shoulder the pack burden of a fellow prisoner, an older and a feeble man.

The band traveled westward to the Genesee. There is a story, possibly legendary, that when the Indians arrived at

46

a village on the site of Nunda, Jones was told that a council had been held and that the Great Spirit had interceded in his behalf.

But still the white youth, whom the Senecas named Hoc-sa-go-wah, "the Handsome Boy," must run the gantlet at the council house at Caneadea, on the Genesee.

The man who had personally taken Jones prisoner came from that important Seneca village. He was a half breed named Jack Berry. Before the raiding party left for Pennsylvania, a Seneca woman at Caneadea, mourning the loss of a son, commissioned Berry to bring her a white captive for adoption. She gave him a string of white wampum to fasten about the prisoner's neck so that she might identify him.

Berry had the bereaved mother in mind when he seized the well-favored Jones and around his prisoner's neck he hung the string of wampum. Fortunately the white youth did not remove it.

In the grim gantlet run at Caneadea, Jones managed to dodge most of the shower of clubs, knives, rocks, and hatchets. Some of his comrades were not so lucky or so agile. The blood of one hapless tomahawked man splashed on Horatio as he neared the council house which was supposed to be sanctuary and the end of the run. But contrary to the rules, a few braves barred its door.

One of them was young Sharp Shins who bore Jones a grudge because the white captive had beaten him in a foot race. Sharp Shins threw his tomahawk at close range but Jones ducked in time, then darted into the nearest Indian cabin. It chanced to be the home of the woman who had wanted a white foster son. She saw the white wampum around Jones' neck and she hid him from his pursuers.

After the ordeal by gantlet, Horatio was adopted into the

47

tribe and given much freedom. Once he ran away. But after being out on the trail one night, his conscience smote him. He was not playing square with the Indians who had trusted him. So back to the lodge he went—to stay with the Senecas until he was released after the Treaty of Fort Stanwix in 1784.

The Indians admired his spirit. When they threw hatchets at him, he hurled them back. Often his aim was better. One young brave began to amuse himself at Jones' expense shortly after the white boy joined the tribe. Horatio warned him to desist. The brave kept up his horse play. At meal time one day Jones jumped up, ran to the fire, seized a boiling squash by the neck, chased and caught his tormentor. Then he thrust the hot squash between the Indian's loose garments and his bare skin. After that he was let alone.

Another Indian who struck Jones in the face with a bunch of roots received a blow from the white prisoner's fist that broke the Seneca's nose and he went through the rest of life with a deformed nasal organ.

Jones made himself useful to the Indians by repairing their hunting weapons. He resolved their quarrels and they came to heed the advice of "The Handsome Boy." And what was important to him and to the Senecas in later years, the prisoner became adept in the tribal language.

As time went on, more white prisoners joined the band. Jones managed to save some of them from death or torture. And after his release, he married one fellow captive, Sarah Whitmore. He had met her around Seneca Lake where she had been taken by Mohawk captors and Jones saved her from a forced marriage to an Indian. After her death he married Elizabeth Starr, 12 years his junior. He begot 16 children by his two wives.

His life was a succession of adventures and exploits. The Indians believed the Tonawanda Creek was haunted by witches and that no one had ever swum the stream and lived. At a time of high water they wanted a canoe that was on the opposite shore and Jones offered to swim across the creek and get it. The horrified Senecas sought to dissuade him from what they thought was suicide.

Then up spake the bold Horatio, in the spirit of the Horatius who guarded the bridge that led to ancient Rome:

"I come of a people that has control over the witches of the waters."

He swam back with the canoe and the Indians were much impressed. They believed Jones was possessed of supernatural powers.

A British officer at Fort Niagara wanted to buy the white prisoner from his foster parents and displayed gold pieces as he bragged of the vast riches of his father, the King. He got this curt answer:

"Go tell your father, the King, he is not rich enough to buy Hoc-sa-go-wah, the Handsome Boy."

After his release Horatio Jones ran a trading post on the site of the present village of Waterloo. He was an agent for John Jacob Astor and the fur baron once spent a night with Jones in the Seneca Lake country.

Jones was often delegated to carry money and dispatches for the government. He rode long distances across a thinly-settled frontier on missions that were fraught with danger.

He was commissioned to carry the money from Canandaigua to Buffalo Creek that was to be paid the Senecas for their lands. It was a considerable sum and in specie. Armed with tomahawk, and gun, Jones mounted his horse with this final direction:

49

"If I am murdered you will find the money 20 rods north-west of where I sleep."

Jones made his destination but not without incident. He awoke one night under the stars with the feeling he was being spied upon and arose from his lonely camp fire at dawn. He had gone only a little way down the trail when an Indian sprang from some bushes, brandishing a club. Jones spurred his horse and was soon out of danger. As he looked back over his shoulder, he saw in an opening in the forest a kettle above a blazing fire.

To the end of his days he believed that had he been captured, he would have been consigned to that kettle.

President Washington made Jones official interpreter at treaty councils with the Indians. He was the interpreter at the Treaty of Big Tree in 1797 held on meadowlands under a giant oak west of the present Geneseo. That treaty extinguished the Seneca title to the territory west of the Genesee which Robert Morris had already sold, without the knowledge or consent of the Indians, to the Dutch capitalists of the Holland Land Company.

Jones was the favorite interpreter of the silver-tongued Red Jacket. The Seneca orator's sonorous periods lost nothing in Jones' translations.

At a time when the Indians were unreconciled and wavering in their relations with the white settlers, their former prisoner exercised a beneficent influence with the tribes. He is credited with smoothing over many a difficulty over land and with thwarting some greedy attempts to grab the meager holdings of the once powerful Senecas.

The Senecas reciprocated by giving Jones and another onetime Indian prisoner and trader, Joseph Smith, a large tract in the Town of Leicester.

50

In 1790 a few weeks before the Wadsworth brothers, James and William, came to the Genesee Valley, Horatio Jones and his brother, John H., left Geneva and followed the main Indian trail through Canandaigua and Avon, with a cart, their families and their household belongings.

That cart was the first wheeled vehicle over the road that is now Routes 5 and 20. In 1790 there was no path from Avon to Leicester. The Joneses picked their way over the ridges and through the openings.

The place where Horatio Jones settled is still known as Jones Bridge. There in 1796 he built the first frame building in the township. It was a barn. His log house had to suffice as a residence for the time being.

The Indians did not forget their friend. In 1798 the Senecas asked the New York Legislature to grant Jones and Jasper Parrish of Canandaigua, whose career in many ways paralleled the bold Horatio's, land along the Niagara River near Black Rock, now an important part of industrial Buffalo. Farmer's Brother eulogized the two former captives of his people in these words:

"As the Whirlwind (the Revolution) was so directed to throw into our arms two of your children, we adopted them into our families and made them *our* children. We loved them and nourished them. They lived with us many years. Then they left us. We wished them to return and promised to each a tract of land and now we wish to fulfill the promise we made them and reward them for their services."

The Seneca's eloquence was wasted. The former captives did not get the land beside the Niagara. Maybe somebody remembered Jones already had that tract in the Valley.

The former Minute Man became a captain of militia and a patriarchal figure among the pioneers. He had many descendants in the Valley, among them James W. Gerard, who was the United States ambassador to Germany at the outbreak of the first World War and who was born in Geneseo.

Death rang down the curtain on Horatio Jones' adventurous life in 1836. He was 72. He had seen both the wilderness and the Indians tamed.

In Geneseo's old Temple Hill Cemetery, along with the Wadsworth brothers and many another Valley pioneer, sleeps this "Davy Crockett of the Genesee," the one the Senecas named "The Handsome Boy."

*   *   *

Moses Van Campen was the Seneca's "Enemy Number One." Far and wide he was known during the Revolution as "the Injun Killer."

His friend, Horatio Jones, won and held the friendship of the Indians. But to Major Moses Van Campen, "the only good Injun was a dead Injun." Many a red warrior's scalp dangled from his belt during the years of conflict.

There was reason for his dislike of Indians. He had watched them slay and scalp his father and younger brother. He had seen comrades tortured to death. Himself twice a prisoner of the Senecas, he had survived the savage gantlet. Once he won his liberty by tomahawking to death five sleeping Indians.

While he was a British prisoner at Fort Niagara, the Indians demanded that he be turned over to their tender mercies and they offered 14 prisoners in exchange for "the Injun Killer." The British spared his life by shifting him to a prison in Montreal, much to the wrath of the Redskins.

When an admiring British officer offered him a commission in the army of the King, Van Campen thundered:

52

"Give me the stake, the tomahawk and the scalping knife sooner than a British commission!"

He despised the British because they offered the Indians bounties for white scalps and because they encouraged bloody raids on helpless border settlements.

So it was little wonder that Moses Van Campen became a sort of legend in the Genesee Country, that he was venerated above the run of Revolutionary veterans and was honored at patriotic gatherings for years. He was 92 when death finally claimed him at his home in Dansville in the year of 1849.

He was born in New Jersey in 1757 of Dutch-French parentage. He spent most of his childhood in Pennsylvania in the Delaware Water Gap country. His mother taught him until he was nine. Then he attended district school.

Moses showed early talent for leadership in the games of boyhood. He shot his first deer when he was 15 years old. At an early age he learned the fundamentals of the surveyor's profession.

When he was 17 the Van Campens moved to a really wild frontier, Pennsylvania's Wyoming Valley. That valley became the scene of a land war between Pennsylvanians and Connecticut settlers and later of ghastly massacre of settlers by Indians and British.

As he expressed it in later years, Moses Van Campen was "nurtured by the school of the rifle and the tomahawk" on a blood-stained frontier. He grew into a powerful man, 5 feet 10 inches tall, a crack shot and a skilled woodsman.

When the Revolution came, he served as lieutenant of local troops protecting the settlements in the region and as commander of one fort repulsed an attack by means of a cleverly built barricade of brush and stakes.

Van Campen distinguished himself by leading five men on a raid upon a house where five Tories had barricaded themselves. He ordered his men to batter down the door with an oak ram, then he sprang through the opening to face the Tories with rifles cocked. One muzzle was thrust in his face. He batted it down just as it exploded. It burned off the hair at his temple and left a permanent scar. Van Campen seized the man who had fired at him. Each of his men tackled a Tory. Each subdued his man in a fierce struggle.

He was a quartermaster in the punitive expedition that Gen. John Sullivan led against the Seneca homeland in 1779 but the routine of collecting and distributing supplies was not to his liking.

Van Campen saw plenty of action when the army entered the Chemung Valley. His scouting party was ambushed near the present village of Chemung. Six of his men were killed and nine wounded. He ordered his men to take cover and lie quietly until the Senecas, thinking they were safe, came out for the scalps of the dead and the dying. Then the withering American fire nearly wiped out the enemy force.

Two days later Van Campen was fighting with Parr's riflemen in the battle of Newtown, the decisive engagement of the Sullivan campaign. Crouched behind a stump during the thick of that battle, he noted that several balls were coming uncomfortably close to him. Finally he spotted the Indian sharpshooter up a tree. He took careful aim and the marksman dropped like a stricken squirrel.

Van Campen did not know—or much care—whether he had killed his man or merely maimed him. Years later a chief named Shongo came to the Van Campen residence at Angelica and showed the scar on his hip that he bore as a souvenir of the battle of Newtown.

It was in 1780 that a band of Indians surprised Van Campen, his father and a younger brother in the dooryard of their home. Moses had to stand by while the savages killed his father and brother with spears, then took their scalps. He saved his own life by hiding every trace of emotion despite his inner anguish and horror. The Indians held stoicism in high esteem.

Van Campen became their prisoner, along with two other white men, Pence and Pike. The trio hatched a plan to escape. While their 10 guards were sleeping, Van Campen and Pike would fall upon them with tomahawks and Pence with gunfire. But at night their feet were tied.

One night an Indian inadvertently dropped a knife near Van Campen who slyly kicked it into the dirt to hide it. When the guards were asleep, he retrieved the knife, took it to Pence and the trio's bonds were cut.

At the critical moment Pike flunked and did nothing. But Van Campen killed five of the Indians with a tomahawk and Pence accounted for four others with his rifle. The tenth Redskin escaped after a fierce tussle with Van Campen. The three white men were in possession of 12 guns, several blankets and nine scalps. After that they called Moses Van Campen "the Injun Killer" and his name was a feared and hated one in the Seneca Nation.

Back in the Wyoming Valley, he led several forays against lurking Indian and Tory bands. Once Van Campen and a comrade disguised themselves as Indians and successfully raided an enemy camp. His collection of scalps grew.

In 1782 his scouting party of 20 men was surprised by 85 whooping Senecas. The outnumbered survivors of the ambuscade surrendered. Van Campen again was a prisoner. But the Indians did not know his identity. Otherwise he would have been excuted—after appropriate torture.

Van Campen saw the Indians butcher four of his comrades. When a Seneca was about to finish off a wounded man named Burwell with his hatchet, Van Campen sprang forward, struck the brave in the chest and sent him reeling to the ground.

What followed is told in this fashion in a rare little book titled *Sketches of Border Adventures in the Life and Times of Moses Van Campen,* written in 1842 by the veteran's grandson, John N. Hubbard:

"The warriors then turned their hatchets upon Van Campen. But a part who had witnessed the scene were highly pleased with the bravery that had been shown by their prisoner and as the tomahawk was gleaming over his head, they leaped forward to rescue him from death. For a few moments Van Campen could hear nothing but the clashing of tomahawks as the warriors engaged in a fierce struggle for his life. . . . At length the fortune of the contest turned in his favor, the majority being determined to spare his life."

For good measure the Indians treated and cured Burwell's wound.

The prisoners were marched off toward Niagara. Along the way they were joined by another group of captives that included Horatio Jones, the interpreter. Jones recognized "the Injun Killer" but protected his identity.

At Caneadea the whites had to run the gantlet. Van Campen dodged and ducked his way to the council house. Only two squaws, armed with clubs, stood in his path. He sent one reeling with a straight arm jab and he kicked the other in the stomach. The watching Indians guffawed and bothered Van Campen no more.

Only after he had been turned over to the British at Niagara did the Indians know they had had "the Injun Killer" in their hands. Then came the offer of 14 prisoners for him and the merciful transfer to Montreal prison.

Van Campen eventually was paroled and returned to Pennsylvania where the end of the war found him a major in command of Wilkes-Barre fort.

He became one of the first settlers in the new Genesee Country. When Charles Williamson, the land agent, was building towns and roads in the wilderness, Van Campen was his chief surveyor. He served Philip Church, the father of Allegany County, in a like capacity and early in the 19th Century took up residence in Angelica, the village that Judge Church had named after his mother and had made the shire town.

Van Campen was an early judge and treasurer of Allegany County. A creek in the center of the county still bears his name and there are many descendants of the Revolutionary hero living in Western New York.

In the late years of his life he resided at Dansville. When the remains of Boyd and Parker and the other victims of the 1779 ambuscade of Groveland Hill were brought to Rochester's Mount Hope Cemetery for re-interment, it was 84-year-old Moses Van Campen, veteran of the Sullivan Expedition, who presided at the exercises.

The Tennessee hills have no monopoly on "kings of the wild frontier." The Genesee Valley had its Davy Crocketts in Horatio Jones and Moses Van Campen.

Chapter 5

The Vision of Handsome Lake

There was a day in 1801 when they thought Handsome Lake was dead. For four years after leaving his native Genesee Valley, he had never left his sick bed in the home of his married daughter on the Cattaraugus Reservation beside the Allegheny River in the shadow of the wild green hills.

He had lived 65 years and most of them had been wasted in dissipation and idleness. Illness had weakened a never robust and much abused body and now Handsome Lake lay as if dead.

The Indians were about to begin the unearthly wailing that would proclaim to the village the death of the highborn sachem of the Turtle Clan, Ga-ni-di-yo, called by the white men Handsome Lake, half brother of Chief Cornplanter and like him a native of Canawaugus, the Seneca village "of the stinking waters," near Avon.

One of the watchers at the bedside touched the wasted frame. His hand found a warm spot. Handsome Lake was not yet ready for the long ride through the stars to the Indian heaven. Yet in reality the old Handsome Lake, the drunken idler, was dead. In his place was born the dedicated Peace Prophet.

Handsome Lake regained consciousness and his lips

moved. He told the Indians of his wondrous vision. In it had appeared four young men like angels. They were the messengers of the Great Spirit and they had revealed to him a new religion which they commanded him to spread among his people.

Swifty he recovered from his illness and as bidden by the angels of his vision, began his preaching mission, going from village to village as the Nazarene had done so long ago.

It was a code of morals rather than a revolutionary new religion that Handsome Lake taught. Despite its spectacular, supernatural origin, it really was a simple set of rules of conduct.

Temperance was the keynote of the crusade of the reformed drunkard. He clearly saw how the white man's firewater had debauched the Indian character, giving birth to two other vices alien to the Indian nature, falsehood and thievery.

Handsome Lake made little headway at first. He met only ridicule and apathy. The Seneca orator, Red Jacket, who distrusted anything new, branded him an imposter. Cornplanter had no faith in his half-brother's revelations. Cornplanter had the same Indian mother as Handsome Lake but the former's father was a white man, John O'Bail.

The Peace Prophet was no magnetic orator, no Billy Sunday or Billy Graham. There was nothing about this aging, sickly Indian to stir the multitude. But he was earnest and he was persistent. And he enlisted eloquent young missionaries to spread the gospel according to Handsome Lake.

Gradually he built up a following, especially among the Senecas and the Onondagas. A feather in his cap was the letter commending his work which Henry Dearborn, secretary of war, wrote at the instance of President Jefferson. That was in 1802 after Handsome Lake had visited the national capital.

The hostility of his half brother drove the crusader to leave the Cornplanter-dominated Cattaraugus Reservation in 1813 to live with the Tonawanda Band beside the Cattaraugus Creek.

No matter where his residence, Handsome Lake never faltered in his mission until death came, on Aug. 10, 1815, in a cabin beside a creek at Onondaga. Knowing his end was near, he had, without telling his disciples, sought that spot only a few days before he left on his journey to that celestial land where only one white man, George Washington, has ever been admitted.

There's a handsome tomb above the grave of the Peace Prophet in the land of the Onondagas near the Long House and the birthplace of the great Confederacy of the Iroquois nations.

The Gai-wii-o, the record of his teachings, still lives. It is recited at nonChristian festivals on the reservations. It was written down in the early years by Chief John Jacket at Cattaragus Reservation. The original copy was lost yet the code was preserved. Chosen preachers had memorized it through several generations.

In the early years of this century, one of them, Edward Cornplanter, wrote it down, in his own language. He was encouraged in this task by the late Dr. Arthur C. Parker, then state archeologist and later director of the Rochester Museum. It was translated by William Bluesky, a lay preacher, and a copy is in the New York State Archives, thanks to Arthur Parker, in whose veins flowed the blood of the Senecas.

Stripped of its mystical touches and some of its prophecies,

61

the Gai-wii-o would be acceptable to any religious or civic group striving for righteousness today.

It condemns drunkenness as "a great and monstrous evil which has reared a high heap of bones." It denounces witchcraft, evil gossip, vanity and false pride. It recognizes the Golden Rule in this phraseology:

"The Creator ordained that human creatures should be kind one to the other and help each other."

The code preaches constancy in marriage, keeping the family together and having large families. Abortion is forbidden. The Prophet loved children and warned against unjust punishment of them. He also urged childless couples to adopt children.

Handsome Lake urged his people to call on the afflicted and decreed no one had any right to demand compensation for treating the sick, a sentiment not endorsed by any medical society. He extolled hospitality to the stranger and the value of occasionally communing with oneself in the wilderness.

On the practical side he abjured the Indians to copy the whites in all progressive ways, to learn the English language, to keep cattle and swine.

A semi-political note is injected into one of his parables. In his vision he sees an Indian chief sweating out an eternal sentence in the Indian Hades. The Prophet is told that unfortunate is the first chief to consent to the sale of Indian lands to a white man.

Although the Christian religion is ignored in the code, Handsome Lake in his vision saw a man with pierced hands and feet who was slain by his own people long ago in a faroff land.

The idea of a human soul and a Supreme Being runs

62

throughout his preaching. The Prophet deplored the Indian worship of animals and urged disbanding of the secret societies with their weird and ancient ritual. The chiefs ordered them dissolved but they merely went underground and still survive on some reservations.

He borrowed some hellfire and brimstone theories from the white preachers, grimly predicting the end of the world in 300 years—by fire. Well, the year 2101 has not dawned yet. Maybe Handsome Lake was a true prophet.

Handsome Lake painted this dire picture of Doomsday: "And not one shall escape for all the world will be enveloped in flames and all those who refuse to believe in Gai-wii-o will be in it."

Somehow it is reminiscent of stiff-necked old Cotton Mather damning all nonconformists in colonial New England and of Herbert Hoover's grim warning that "grass will grow in the streets of your cities" in the Presidential campaign of 1932.

The Prophet deferred to two Indian traditions, the sacrifice of the White Dog on New Years Day and the Thanksgiving festivals. He deplored the old Indian custom of a year's mourning for the departed, declaring ten days of mourning sufficient and that "when a friend departs, lay your grief aside."

It all seems too simple and too lucid, a mere exposition of "the good, the beautiful and the true." But the Indians were a primitive, simple people and the gospel according to Handsome Lake was introduced at a propitious time.

The code had far reaching effects. It rallied and solidified the Iroquois spirit in a time of defeat in war and loss of their homeland. It saved many an Indian from a drunkard's grave. Certainly it effectively arrested the spread of Chris-

63

tianity among the Indians. The strength of the nonChristion party on New York State reservations today springs from the seed so well planted more than 150 years ago by the frail old crusader from Canawaugus, the reformed drunkard who talked with angels.

Chapter 6

Lost City of the Genesee

Williamsburg is just part of the Valley landscape now— 80 acres of pasture and field on the river flats.

Only the old cemetery on the hill behind the spiked iron fence and the historical marker beside the busy highway below it tell of the short-lived glory of "the City of the Genesee."

Williamsburg has been dead these many years. Now even the trees in the old graveyard along the Abell Hill Road are dying. And many of the tombstones of the pioneers long lay tumbled on the ground.

Williamsburg is as if it never was.

Yet before there was a Rochester, a Buffalo or a Syracuse, there was a thriving village at the confluence of the Cana-seraga Creek and the Genesee River three miles south of Big Tree, now Geneseo.

It was the first settlement in what is now Livingston County. It was the scene of the first agricultural fair in Up-state New York.

Williamsburg was born in the busy brain of Charles Williamson, the land agent. In 1792 he founded at the meeting of the waters what he believed would be the commercial center of the rich young Genesee Country.

The greatest real estate salesman of his time was to father other towns, Bath and Sodus Point, and to develop Geneva and Lyons but Williamsburg was the first.

The story of the lost city revolves about the romantic figure of Charles Williamson, the tall Scot in the blue military cloak, the tricorn hat and the powdered wig. It was for less than a decade that he galloped over this frontier but he left the indelible imprint of his personality on the Genesee Country.

He had been reared in aristocratic surroundings in Scotland, the son of the factor for the Earl of Hopetoun. He first landed in America in 1781, in the red coat of a British army captain, a prisoner of war. His ship had been captured on the way.

Williamson was only 24 then. He was housed in the home of a Boston merchant and soon married the merchant's daughter, Abigail Newell. He came to know and like America and American ways.

He possessed the quenchless optimism of the born promoter, along with imagination, daring and vast energy. He was equally at home in drawing room or frontier cabin. He had a charm that few men—and fewer women—could resist.

Such was the magnetic and dashing fellow, who, back in Scotland in 1791, had been chosen as the American agent for a British land syndicate, headed by Sir William Pulteney. This company had bought one million wild Genesee Country acres from that over-extended Philadelphia speculator, Robert Morris, financier of the Revolution. Williamson had become a naturalized American citizen and this wilderness empire was in his name because at the time no foreigner could hold title to American real estate.

To develop this vast tract Williamson projected among

many enterprises a highway from the Susquehanna at North-umberland, Pa., over the mountains to Southern York State and westward to the Genesee.

Early in the Summer of 1792 he came on horseback with a party of scouts to the junction of the Canaseraga and the Genesee. He picked that spot for the northern terminal of his highway.

There in the clearing, where the squaws for years had tilled their gardens before Sullivan drove the Senecas out of their "Pleasant Valley," Williamson visualized a city that would be the meeting place for the trade of East and West.

In his mind's eye he saw streams of boats carrying the wheat, flax and hemp of the river valley to tidewater ports and world markets. Where the forest stood, he saw orchards and wheat fields and great estates in the British pattern.

This was sparsely settled country in 1792. The Wads-worth brothers, after two years in the Valley, were still living in their log cabin at Big Tree northward on the Gen-esee. Much farther north at the falls where Rochester stands today bluff, bigamous Indian Allen was running his lonely grist mill. A few New Englanders were settling Hartford, to be renamed Avon. Nearby were the Indian reservations at Squawkie Hill and Gardeau, the tract of "The White Woman."

Canandaigua and Geneva were the principal communities of the frontier. There were hardly 900 people living west of Seneca Lake when Williamson founded his City of the Gen-esee.

The land agent named his dream city Williamsburg in honor of his principal, Sir William Pulteney. With charac-teristic celerity, he engaged surveyors and builders. He left the actual building of the town to a fellow Scot, John Johnstone, but he watched its progress with an eager eye.

By the Fall of 1792, the outlines of the city of the Genesee began to emerge. Around a central square there arose a row of cabins, a tavern, a frame store, a grist mill, besides the farmhouse and the great L-shaped "Long Barn" of the land agent.

*   *   *

Williamsburg's first settlers were hardly to the fastidious land agent's liking.

The lords of the English syndicate had evolved a rather medieval six-year sharecrop plan for colonizing their Genesee lands. To this end a former picture peddler, an aggressive and plausible chap, one William Berczy, had been commissioned to recruit a band of German farm workers for the enterprise.

Instead of sturdy Saxon peasants born to the soil, Berczy rounded up a motley crew of 60 emigrants from the slums of Hamburg.

On arrival in the new country, they soon proved their utter unfitness for frontier life. Put to work building roads, they proved clumsy, unskilled with ax or saw, and were made the butt of the backwoodsmen's jeers. Finally about 30 of them made their way to the Genesee village John Johnstone had built and they became Williamsburg's first settlers.

Dissension pervaded the settlement from the beginning. Berczy piled up debts against the company. He complained the land agent had violated his contract with the emigrants. The covenant called for houses, lands, live stock and equipment for each settler. There were not nearly enough homes and half of the promised land was pre-empted by Williamson. There were few plows, spinning wheels or other tools. Probably the Germans would not have used them anyhow.

Matters raced to a showdown that Summer of 1793. The land agent was tired of the Germans and their complaints. They were not the type of settlers he wanted in the Genesee Country and their coming had not been of his doing. So he resolved to get rid of them.

Justifying his action by Berczy's debts and errors in his accounts, along with refusal of the Germans to till the lands, the land agent summarily dismissed Berczy as a representative of the company and refused to transfer an acre of land to the Germans.

This ultimatum Williamson coolly delivered in person before a howling mob at Williamsburg. He was driven to cover in a cabin and the cornered land agent escaped bodily harm only through the intercession of Berczy.

After that riotous incident, Williamson acted swiftly. He appealed to the courts for redress and protection. A sheriff's posse raided Williamsburg, rounded up most of the feckless Germans and marched them off to Canandaigua jail.

They were convicted of defrauding the English land company and made to pay off their fines in labor. Eventually most of them found their way to Upper Canada. Thus ingloriously ended the experiment in German colonization in the Valley of the Genesee.

*   *   *

So it was left to the Yankees and the Pennsylvanians, plus a few hardy Scots, to people the growing villiage.

After the departure of the Germans, Williamson lavished money on the city of the Genesee. He added a second story to the tavern for a ball room and community center. He

69

even considered starting a dancing school. He had a black-smith shop and a distillery built. He pampered his pioneers with imported food and drink and the Williamsburgers lived "higher on the hog" than even the prosperous Wadsworth brothers at Big Tree.

In the early Fall of 1793, Williamson launched his most grandiose promotion. He sent out broadsides advertising "the Williamsburg Fair and Races at the Great Forks of the Genesee," to be held two days in late September "for the sale and purchase of cattle, horses and sheep."

It was the first such fair ever held west of the Hudson. The land agent laid out a race track on the flats, spurred his road building, won contributions from James Wadsworth and from Thomas Morris of Canandaigua, son of Robert, and he dipped deeply into company funds to put across his fair.

It was a colorful show in which sporting gentry journeyed from seaboard cities to mingle with the yeomen of the frontier. The crowd looked over the animals, took part in the races and games, wagered heavily and feasted on roast ox. There was liquid refreshment for all. The settlers staged wrestling matches with the Indians. The land agent pronounced his fair a success and charged the cost off to "promotion." Charles Williamson was way ahead of his times.

The Williamsburg Fair was repeated the next season. In 1795 the land promoter shifted the affair to Bath, which had become the apple of his eye, the place of his residence and his headquarters. But he never forgot nor neglected Williamsburg. It had been the first born.

The years 1795–96 saw Williamsburg's heyday. Some 40 houses were grouped around the square. A smithy, a ware-house, a dry goods store were added to the village. Its tavern was noted all over the frontier. Races and fairs were planned at its tables. Costly livestock cavorted in the fields around the "Long Barn."

But evil days faced the City of the Genesee. Williamson's lavish expenditures were to prove his undoing. He is said to have spent one million dollars promoting a country that yielded only $1,000 a month.

He had founded towns and spurred the development of others. He had built roads and schools and established in Bath the first newspaper on the frontier. Only the magnificent land agent would have opened a theater on the backwoods square of Bath that presented the sophisticated plays of Moliere. He opened a grand hotel at Geneva and launched a sloop on Seneca Lake. He brought a group of impecunious fellow Scots as settlers around the Big Springs at Caledonia.

Williamson had unlimited faith in the future of this Genesee Country. But his English principals wanted quick returns on their investment and they saw only the red figures on the ledgers.

So in the year 1801 Charles Williamson, one of the most compelling figures in pioneer history, was discharged and a conservative American, Robert Troup, was named as land agent in his stead.

A Scot had spent too much!

Williamsburg's knell was sounded with Williamson's departure. The land agent died of yellow fever in 1806 aboard a ship bound for the West Indies and was buried at sea.

Troup had none of Williamson's sentiment for Williamsburg nor any confidence in its future. Troup would extend no further aid to its settlers and he looked with disfavor on the Long Barn and other evidences of his predecessor's extravagances and sporting proclivities.

Still the village at the Great Forks of the Genesee did not expire at once. Its life was prolonged by a visit to the Genesee Country of three Marylanders on horseback about the time Williamson was being called to account by his British masters.

The Southerners, men of consequence and property, were Nathaniel Rochester, William Fitzhugh and Charles Carroll. One of Williamson's last and most significant acts was to sell the three men large tracts in the Genesee Valley.

Colonel Rochester settled at Dansville before he went north to found the city that bears his name. Although Carroll and Fitzhugh were associated with him in that venture, they never lived in Rochester but remained to the end of their days on the estates they had bought in the Valley. Carroll's estate was at Williamsburg. Fitzhugh built a noble white pillared house at Hampton Corners, where the Dansville and Mount Morris roads converge.

Despite their efforts to keep Williamsburg alive, the village was fading fast. Settlers began to move out. Soon the great Long Barn was mouldering into ruins. The deserted tavern with its elaborate ball room went up in flames. Grass covered the race track.

Williamsburg had long been overshadowed by the Wadsworths' village of Big Tree—which became Geneseo. The Carrolls and Fitzhughs, hoping to save Williamsburg, presented its claims as the county seat when Livingston County was formed in 1821. It was far too late. Williamsburg's star had set. The powerful Wadsworths saw to it that Geneseo became the shire town.

Fire long ago took the mansion of the Carrolls and in this

72

century the Abell residence on the hill near the cemetery suffered the same fate.

In the old graveyard sleeps the most picturesque of the Abells, David H., "The Genesee Farmer." He was a political lieutenant of Whig Boss Thurlow Weed and a crafty one. In financial affairs he was not so astute. He named the driveway in front of his house after a local sheriff because, 'tis said, of that official's frequent trips there on behalf of "the Farmer's" creditors. Abell died in 1872.

Now no vestige is left of the city at the Greak Forks except the cemetery on the hill. There has not been a burial there in years.

Many tombstones lay flat on the ground in the Summer of 1955. Others tilted at crazy angles. But still erect were the plain white stones at the graves of two of Rochester's founders, William Fitzhugh and Charles Carroll. Recently all the stones were restored to upright positions. There are proud names upon them.

One is that of Samuel Adams Lee, son of Richard Henry Lee of Virginia and the only Lee to fight against the South in the Civil War. He was a captain in the Federal Navy and was allied by marriage to the Carrolls.

The tallest shaft of all bears a once famous name, that of James G. Birney (1792–1857). He was twice the nominee of the Liberty (Anti-Slavery) Party for President of the United States in the 1840s and the leader of the Constitutional Abolitionists, although he once had owned slaves. Birney was born in Kentucky and died in New Jersey. He never lived in the Genesee Valley but he married a Fitzhugh.

There are humble names on the stones, too. One is that of "Mammy Rachel, 96." Another stone is inscribed "Aunt

73

Katie." Probably they were old retainers of the landed gentry, two of the slaves Birney worked so hard to free.

Cemeteries are not lively places. The one on the hill above the Geneseo-Mount Morris road is especially quiet. Only the murmur of the motor traffic below, the song of the birds or the tinkle of a cow bell breaks the ghostly silence there. The only permanent living thing is the myrtle which spread its blue-green carpet on the earth in the Spring. Even the trees are dying in Williamsburg cemetery.

And they say—and of course it is sheer fantasy—that on soft moonlight nights a tall figure astride a noble chestnut horse comes galloping down the Valley road like the wind. The spectral rider wears a blue cloak and a tricorn hat. He reins in his steed where the waters of the Genesee and Canaseraga unite. It is Charles Williamson, the land agent, looking for his City of the Genesee.

Chapter 7

Avon Spa

Avon water, bluish, pungent and not ill tasting, has gushed out of the flatlands from the beginning.

Across the river from the Indian village of Canawaugus, which in the Seneca tongue means "stinking waters," were —and still are—the mineral springs which once made Avon a little Saratoga.

Canawaugus lay on the main trail from the Hudson to Lake Erie and the fame of the healing waters spread throughout the forest empire of the Iroquois. Many an ailing brave came to quaff of the stinking waters and to bathe in the springs.

Avon, always the place on the main trails where the traveler has found food and drink and shelter, thus was catering to the "tourist trade" long before the white man came to the Valley.

In the days of French domination, the powerful and diplomatic Joncaire the elder and the Jesuit missionaries knew of the mineral springs and of the veneration in which the Senecas held them.

And when the first white settlers came, they found a well-worn trail leading to the springs from the main Indian highway and they learned from the Senecas of the magic powers of the waters.

75

Here is a word picture of the springs in the early time from Turner's *History of the Phelps and Gorham Purchase:*

". . . they were surrounded by a dense cedar marsh. The waters of the spring flowed into a basin or pool covering several acres, the margin of which was pure white sand, thrown up by the action of the waters. The water was clear and transparent and shaded by the dark forest, the spot had a mild and romantic aspect."

It still has, although the dark forest and the sand-bordered pond are long gone and the great flocks of wild pigeons no longer roost there as they did in the time of the pioneers. But the pungent odor of the mineral springs still affronts the nostrils as of old.

The white settlers observed that sick hogs would roll in the mud of the sulphur waters. A skin disease known as the "Genesee Itch" afflicted the porkers of the frontier. It plagued the settlers, too, according to Turner, who neglected to state whether they caught it from the hogs or vice versa.

It came about that a Miss Wemple, sister of an Avon pioneer, who suffered from a "wasting disease," not the "Genesee Itch," bathed in the spring, drank the waters and was relieved. Other similar cases spread the fame of the springs and visitors began coming there in considerable numbers after the War of 1812.

Richard Wadsworth, son of Gad, an early settler, owned the land around the Lower Spring, largest of the five in the vicinity. In 1821 this sagacious Wadsworth, a distant kinsman of James and William, cleared the place with shovel and ax and erected a rude wooden "showering box" where mineral baths might be taken—at a price. It was the dawning era of the water cure in America and Wadsworth was the first to sense the commercial possibilities of the ill-smelling waters going to waste on the Avon flats.

Out of Richard Wadsworth's pioneer "shower bath" grew Avon Spa, in its time one of the most fashionable watering places in the East, with big wooden hotels, bath houses, landscaped gardens and sylvan walks.

There also was a fine race track, along with bowling alleys, shooting galleries, and a community amusement center called the Pavilion. For many came to the Springs seeking relaxation as well as health. Predominant among such gentry were rich Southerners—before the Civil War.

Big hotels rose in adjacent Avon village. The biggest was the United States, which sprawled over nearly a whole block at the top of Main Street hill. At one time there were 14 hotels at the Springs and in the village.

The year 1828 saw the beginning of the two earliest and most noted hotels at the Springs. One, built near the junction of River and Spring Streets at the entrance to the watering place, was a boarding house in the beginning. Nehemiah Houghton built it and called it the American.

In 1859 it was renamed Congress Hall. It was a ritzy place in its heyday with its own bath house near the Upper Spring and an ornate sunken garden where there is a stagnant pool today. Congress Hall long outlived Avon's reign as a spa. It was razed about 1913.

A young physician named Derick Knickerbocker helped build with his own hands the big hotel with the roomy verandas which he named Knickerbocker Hall. It rose near the Lower Spring, largest of the five in the vicinity, and near the half-mile race track which is still there.

Doctor Knickerbocker fostered the belief that merely breathing the sulphur laden air at the Springs would restore health. There is a story about a wealthy Southern planter holding a tarnished timepiece in his hand and the genial doctor trying to convince his guest that the sulphur fumes blackened his treasured silver watch overnight.

A later owner of Knickerbocker Hall was a picturesque character, Dr. L. G. Smedley. He was called "the Indian Doctor" because it was his custom when faced with a difficult diagnosis to go into a trance, calling for help from the spirit of an Indian medicine man named Wahoo to whom the doctor spoke in a strange tongue. Doctor Smedley sold a "Wahoo Indian Specific" which he claimed would cure fever and other ills. Scoffers said the nostrum was made from cheap whiskey, quinine and plain water, plus certain herbs which the medico made a great show of collecting in the swamps around Avon.

Flames devoured stately Knickerbocker Hall in 1886, a fate shared by so many big wooden hotels at so many resorts.

A key figure in the early development of Avon Springs was a colorful former sea captain who rode a white horse named Pomp. His name was Capt. Asa Knowlen. This Connecticut Yankee was the skipper of a merchantman seized by the French who interned him in the West Indies.

He came to the Genesee Country to operate stage and mail routes and in 1836 bought from Richard Wadsworth 100 acres including the Upper and Lower Springs. He laid out the celebrated race track that same year. For years that track was known as Congress Park. Now it is Avon Springs Downs.

Asa Knowlen built a bottling plant at the Lower Spring and shipped bottles of Avon water, packed in hay, all over the world, even to China. The venture failed, principally because the water would not keep well as it underwent chemical changes when exposed to air and light.

At one time the Knowlen family owned both the United States Hotel uptown and Congress Hall at the Springs and ran hacks night and day between the two hotels, a half mile apart. Congress Park also for years was operated by the Knowlens.

Avon's first settler was a tavern keeper. Playing Mine Host is more than a tradition in this "Northern Bluegrass" community. It is bred in its very bones. The first tavernkeeper was Gilbert Berry and he opened his log inn beside the river in 1789.

But the most famous early inn of Avon was the Hosmer Stand, built by the first James Wadsworth in 1806. It was kept by Dr. Timothy Hosmer, who also was a physician and a judge. He was one of five Connecticut men who bought the site of Avon township, first named Hartford, in 1789. The doctor-hotel keeper wore the powdered wig, deerskin breeches, silver buckles and courtly manners of the Revolutionary era. The Indians called him "Big Fire" because of the great flames that roared on chilly nights in the fireplace of the Hosmer Stand.

To that frontier tavern in the early times came such notables as General Winfield Scott, Joseph Bonaparte, brother of Napoleon and one time king of Spain; Louis Philippe, destined to become a king of France; the French marshal, Grouchy, and many more.

It was on the site of the Hosmer Stand that Asa Knowlen built a frame building in 1836, which, through the years and many additions, became the immense United States Hotel. After the Civil War it was Avon's most famous hostelry. The Saratoga-like structure was destroyed on the night of Feb. 22, 1874 in Avon's greatest fire.

An Avon Springs hotel with a brief history was the Argyle

on River Street nearly opposite Congress Hall. It was built in 1859, for a time was known as Southworth's boarding house and it went up in flames in 1863.

An almost forgotten early hotel was the one operated by Doctor Long at Long's Spring, one mile southwest of the present Avon Springs Downs. There also was a Magnesium Spring west of the driving park and along the river.

The flood tide of the Spa's popularity were those years just before the Civil War, when Southern planters, their families, Negro slaves and sleek horses came to the Northern water cure to escape the Southern summers.

It was a glamorous picture at the Springs those days—the Southern patricians swarming the spacious verandas, the men in long tailed coats of the finest broadcloth, big hats, flowing ties, mirror-bright boots and lemon-colored gloves; their ladies in hoop skirts, silks and velvets that trail the floor, in shawls and bonnets. They carry parasols, for a Southern lady's complexion most never know the fierce rays of the sun. And when the music of the dance sounds, they wear roses in their hair. They sing the new tunes, "Listen to the Mocking Bird" and "Darling Nellie Gray."

The soft drawling Southern voices are heard around the backgammon, whist and chess tables, in the bowling halls, the shooting galleries, in the bars where corks pop from champagne bottles and wagers are laid on the horses that will race at Congress Park.

Although canal packet boats began running through the Valley in 1840 and a railroad nosed into Avon in 1853, the Southerners usually came to the Springs by private carriage. At the Spa they went on horseback rides in the Valley and on excursions by stage coach or chaise to the falls of Portage, to Rochester and to try their fishing luck at Conesus Lake.

Those years just before the Civil War when the Spa enjoyed the generous patronage from Dixie were the gayest in its history.

And after the war clouds had spilled out their four-year rain of death and destruction, Avon Springs was never the same again. The rich Southerners came no more to the big hotels with the roomy verandas. For one thing, they weren't rich any more and even had they somehow kept their money, they would not have spent it again among the "dam Yanks."

Still Avon kept going as a health resort for many years, not on the old lavish scale and with a quieter tone. Several hotels were built after the Civil War, among them the Avon Cure on Wadsworth Avenue, then Cure Street, near the Springs. Charles Whalley erected the four-story building which had rooms for 100 guests and two sulphur springs right on the premises.

In 1871 the Cure was leased to new operators and it got a new name, the Sanitarium. One of its later proprietors was the "Indian Doctor," L. G. Smedley. The building was taken down in 1904. Each board was carefully marked and shipped by railroad to Lakeville, thence by Conesus Lake steamboat to McPherson's Point. There the structure was reassembled into the present Livingston Inn.

Some old registers of the Avon Cure of the 1870s and 1880s are preserved in the Livingston County Historical Museum at Geneseo. Many guests signed from Rochester and other nearby places. Many others came to the water cure from New England and the East. The Middle West is well represented. There are some entries from Canada and a few from the West Coast.

One guest came from Finland, then as now a part of Russia; another was a Chinese. A handful of Kentuckians and

81

West Virginians wrote their names on the old registers—but none from the Deep South, the Land of Cotton through which one William Tecumseh Sherman had marched a few years before.

Catching the eye of the visitor to Avon today are the Saratoga-like proportions of the sprawling Livingston House which faces the village park with the Civil War monument in its center. It began in 1861 as a two-story business block built by William Nesbit. In 1878 it was made into a health resort and enlarged to its present bulk. In its palmy days it had its own bath house, bowling alley and sulphur well. It still caters to the local and the tourist trade, a landmark of the northernmost Valley town.

In 1831 Jonathan Gerry of Massachusetts built a noble pillared residence at Main and Temple Streets. Fifty-one years later Dr. Cyrus Allen and James D. Carson, Sr., bought the mansion, added a third story and opened a sanitarium there. It had its own mineral well in the back yard. For a time they also operated a private bank in the building. It survives today, a gracious white-clad reminder of the good taste of the pioneer builders, as the Avon Inn, known to thousands of tourists on the road across the state.

Another hotel, first named the Avon and later Radford Hall, was built at the park circle during the railroad boom of the late 1850s. It was razed in 1930.

Avon still has a St. George Hotel although two hostelries on its site burned down. The St. George, while never associated closely with the water cure era, figured in a dramatic attempt to revive the old sport of coaching in the 1890s.

Emmett Jennings launched the venture, driving his coach and six horses between the St. George and the Powers Hotel in Rochester over the River Road by way of Scottsville.

Relays of fresh horses were kept at Scottsville and at Dumpling Hill. The countryside gaped at the magnificent coach and six but the venture proved unprofitable, even at $5 per round trip, and was soon abandoned.

Before we turn the page on the story of Avon as a watering place, let's look at the old Springs through the eyes of one who lived there as a boy and later worked in the big wooden hotels.

Samuel Harman is dead now but 13 years ago when I talked with him at his Rochester home and he was in his 80s, he drew on his remarkable memory for a picture of the Springs in their days of glory.

His father managed the Congress Hall bath house for the Knowlens after the Civil War and Sam Harman was brought up amid the bustle and the gayety of a fashionable watering place, although the Southern gentry no longer came to Avon Spa.

Of all the notable guests at the big hotels, the figure most vivid in his memory was that of Cyrus McCormick, the harvester magnate.

One day when the senior Harman dunned the millionaire for a bath house fee, McCormick flew into a rage and struck the manager with his cane. It was not a hard blow and Harman hardly felt it. But his son, as an old man, still remembered the vengeful joy that surged within him when a stone, hurled with all the force of a young body burning with anger over the affront to a well-loved parent, struck a certain harvester king squarely in the back.

There was a summer day in his youth when triple tragedy struck at the park. Dr. Oren Phelps, proprietor of Congress Hall, was having a well drilled near the hotel. The first workman who went down failed to come up and another

83

was lowered into the well to investigate. When nothing was heard from him, a third man went down. None of the trio came out alive. The noxious sulphur gases in the well had taken all three lives.

As a lad in his teens, Samuel Harman worked as a bell boy and handy man at the United States Hotel uptown. The great rambling place was lighted by oil lamps and candles. There were hundreds of them to clean and the old gentleman particularly recalled the pewter candle sticks he had to polish.

He was staying in the hotel the night it burned in 1874 and with hundreds of others watched the leaping flames race through the huge wooden structure. It was a spectacle not soon to be forgotten and for years Avon people dated events as before or after "the big fire."

*　　*　　*

By the mid 1880s the star of Avon Springs as a watering place had set. Knickerbocker Hall burned in 1886. Congress Hall steadily went downhill. The Springs became a picnic ground and meeting place for people of the Valley and attracted few from far places. But there still was racing on the Congress Park track where in 1866 the great Dexter had hung up a world's record, a mile in 2:31.

Around the turn of the century came a new era for the Springs. It became an amusement resort. The Erie ran long excursion trains on week ends from Rochester and other points. A long platform was erected at the Spring Street crossing for the excursion crowds. The German societies of Rochester favored Congress Park for their Sunday outings and in the excursion train which brought these hearty people there was always one car filled with kegs of lager.

But after the horseless carriage and the paved roads changed a people's way of life, the Springs went back to sleep, underbrush grew high around the mineral springs where once had been formal gardens and grass even crept over the race track. Around 1913 Congress Hall, which had been unused for years, was razed, along with the Pavilion, the old community gathering place.

It was Mrs. Herbert Wadsworth of Ashantee, one of the leading horsewomen of America, who in 1914 sparked a movement to rehabilitate the Springs. The property had belonged to the Wadsworths since the 1890s and as long as she lived, Mrs. Wadsworth never gave up her dream of restoring the park to something of its oldtime glory.

Mrs. Wadsworth inspired a meeting in the Summer of 1914 at which a committee headed by Col. Nathan C. Shiverick, manager of Ashantee Farms, organized a community bee to clean up the old park.

On Aug. 1, 1914 the Springs hummed with its oldtime activity. Two hundred men and 40 teams cleared away the tangle of weeds and groomed the old race track. The Springs were spick and span again and after the job was done, Mrs. Wadsworth had a supper served to all hands.

The refurbished grounds was the scene in September, 1914, of the first annual Genesee Valley Fair. Grandstands and other buildings were put up and in 1916 the event was renamed the Livingston County Fair. It was an annual event in the Valley until it gave up the ghost in 1923.

Ever since the organization in 1915 of the Genesee Valley Breeders Association, with Mrs. Wadsworth leading the movement, horse shows have been held in that part of Avon Springs, which includes the race track and is now called Avon Springs Downs. The breeders' association was formed

85

to raise hunters in the Genesee Valley and to generally improve the breed.

Mrs. Wadsworth interested the famous Jockey Club of New York in the enterprise. The club for years has maintained Lookover, a stallion station on the Avon-Geneseo Road, overlooking a broad sweep of Valley. Some famous sires have stood there, including the great Omaha, after his racing days were done. Omaha in 1936 swept the three big races, the Preakness, the Kentucky Derby and the Belmont. Colts bred in the Valley in recent years have taken honors at Saratoga and other notable shows.

The Spring and Fall breeders' shows at Avon Springs Downs are red-letter events in the equine world. Valley-raised hunters and jumpers vie with some of the best in the East.

Visitors to the Springs these days come upon a neat headstone near the wooden canopy which shelters the main or Lower Spring. It bears this inscription:

IMP. TOURIST 2nd
1925–1952
Son-in-Law-Touraine

It stands at the grave of a great stud, Imported Tourist, offspring of Son-in-Law and Touraine. It was erected by the Jockey Club shortly after the horse's death in 1952.

The park was occupied in the early 1940s by the Circle B. Ranch, which operated it as an amusement resort with all kinds of riding devices. The mechanical "rides" were incongruous at the place which all its life had known the flying feet of horses and they didn't last long.

The Springs was the hub of another kind of ride in the early 1920s, an annual five-day Endurance Run which

Congress Hall Hotel in Avon Springs Heyday

THE MONSTER SERPENT OF SILVER LAKE

Sea Serpent Scare as Artist of 1855 Saw It

brought to the Valley many Army Cavalrymen, Western cowboys and horsemen from all over the land. Each day the 60-mile route was changed. The run tested the endurance of both horses and riders for it led over steep hills and rough roads. A blacksmith and a veterinary were part of the retinue and farmers used to have pails of water scattered along the route for thirsty steeds.

Among the entrants in the Endurance Run of October, 1923, was a thin-faced, thin-bodied, smooth shaven Cavalry major from Fort Myer, Va. His fellow officers called him "Skinny." He had been a Cavalryman in World War I and he was an accomplished horseman. But the third day his mount developed a limp and "Skinny" was out of the contest.

"Skinny" was Jonathan Mayhew Wainwright, one of the heroes of the Second World War, the defender of Bataan and the long-time prisoner of the Japanese.

In 1936 a state legislative committee investigated the possibility of developing the several mineral springs in New York. Assemblyman James J. (Jerry) Wadsworth headed the group and you may be sure that Avon Springs in his home Valley got consideration. Some folks had visions of the Springs being restored to their old place among the nation's spas. But in the end nothing came of it. Avon Springs went back to sleep, awakening only for the occasional glitter of the breeders' shows.

The ghostly glade of "the stinking waters" has many rich memories—of the big hotels and the stylish guests, the excursion crowds, the county fair and its midway.

They are all gone. Only the pungent smell of the mineral waters is the same. And there always were and still are horses at the Springs. They come whinnying to the pasture rail these days. And in fancy you see Captain Knowlen there, astride white Pomp, looking over the new half-mile track he laid out. And you hear the quick thud of Dexter's flying feet, setting a new world's record—and the roar of the crowds.

Chapter 8

The Sea Serpent

In the hills of southeastern Wyoming County, only a few miles from the great gorge of the Genesee, lies a sheet of placid water nearly four miles long and three quarters of a mile wide. Its glistening sheen on some moonlight night long ago impelled some pioneer to name it Silver Lake.

The Indians knew it well. There is a legend they shunned it because they believed there was a monster in its depths. But white men have fished and swum there for many a year. Thousands of picnickers and cottagers have frolicked on its shores. And once a veritable little Chautauqua Assembly flourished there.

Its greatest fame came just 100 years ago. Then the fierce white light of national notoriety beat upon the tranquil, hill-girt lake—for a little time.

On the night of July 13, 1855 four men of the community and two young boys climbed into a rowboat with their fishing paraphernalia for an evening of sport. There was no liquor aboard. The men in the boat were temperate, substantial men.

The men were Charles Hall, Joseph R. McKnight, Charles and Alonzo Scribner and the boys were George Hall and John Scribner.

Within an hour they were rowing frantically to shore, white-faced as if the devil himself were at their stren. The story they gasped out shattered the calm of Silver Lake for weeks, sent thousands flocking to its shores and gave birth to a legend.

It was Joe McKnight who saw it first. He took it to be a large log floating on the lake not far from shore. He mentioned it to his companions. To their amazement the object began to move slowly—and toward them.

As it neared their boat, they saw it was a great reptile, 80 feet long, with bright red eyes in a head 15 inches in diameter and with a mighty lashing tail. As they gazed, the creature's mouth squirted water four feet high in the air. It was then the fishermen started rowing like mad for shore, the monster rising at intervals in their wake.

The story spread like wildfire through the countryside. Next night four youths bathing in the lake saw the thing. An old Indian added a supernatural note by relating how his forefathers who lived on Squawkie Hill never fished in Silver Lake because it was haunted by a demon. The fishermen and others made sworn affidavits to having seen the monster.

The local newspapers ran the strange story and soon it was being carried over the wires to all parts of the world. People began pouring in by rail, by canal boat, by horse and carriage, by stage, on foot. The hotels around the lake and in the nearby village of Perry were crammed to the eaves and private homes went into the tourist business. It was a time of real prosperity, as well as real terror, for the community.

A committee of vigilantes was formed to capture the great snake. A tower was erected at the north end of the lake and a sentinel with a spy glass put on around-the-clock duty in it. Hunters armed to the teeth swarmed the shores of Silver Lake. Two of them got distant shots at the creature.

Several well-manned boats went out on the lake hunting the monster. One of them carried Daniel Smith, a native son recently returned from a whaling voyage, and harpoons, lances, coils of rope and other whaling equipment. Smith got within 40 feet of his quarry but the thing glided away and submerged.

Set lines, made of clothes lines, and an enormous iron hook, made by a blacksmith, were put out into the water, baited with ducks, chickens, fresh pork and other delicacies. It was all in vain. The terror grew when a farmer reported a steer missing in the marshes around the lake. The country folk believed the great reptile had seized the animal.

Desperate citizens organized a stock company called the Experiment Corporation to finance the hunt and were about to import a deep sea diver when, as the excitement reached its zenith, the monster vanished from the lake.

Slowly the tumult died and the stream of visitors stopped. But for many a day fishermen and bathers shunned the waters which had housed the terror.

Two years later came the denouement. Fire swept the Walker House, a leading hotel in Perry. When volunteers, trying to save property, forced their way into the attic of the hotel, they came upon a curious thing. It was a huge strip of canvas made into the shape of a serpent and painted a dull green with bright yellow spots. Its eyes and mouth were a brilliant red. The firemen let the fire devour it.

Flames had done what human ingenuity and vigilance could not do. It had fathomed the mystery of the Silver Lake Sea Serpent.

Then the whole story came out. Business had been woefully slack that early summer of 1855 at the lake and A. B. Walker, an enterprising hotel man, hit upon a scheme to pep it up. He confided in a little group of friends. Night after night they worked in an old tannery in a ravine along the lake Outlet, putting Walker's idea into tangible form.

Painstakingly they built the great serpent out of waterproof canvas, supported on the inside by coiled wires, then painted it in fear-provoking hues. They dug a trench and laid a gas pipe in it from the basement of a shanty on the west shore. In the shanty they set up a bellows like that used by a blacksmith and connected it with a small light rubber hose that ran through the pipe from the shanty to the body of the serpent.

One night they took the creature of their creation out from its hiding place and sank it in the lake. A man in the shanty operated the bellows which forced the air into the snake, causing it to rise to the surface. Weights were attached to different parts of the body to insure its sinking as the air was allowed to escape. Ropes were tied to forward parts of the body, extending to three different points on the shore so that the monster could be propelled in any direction desired.

The conspirators made a successful midnight experiment. They watched the head of their monster rise gracefully to a height of about eight feet above the water as other parts of the long body became visible. The bellows-hose contraption worked perfectly.

Then on the night of July 13, 1855, the plotters saw a boat-load of fisherman going out on to the lake and decided it was time to launch their great hoax.

But they found they had built a "Frankenstein" and were soon dismayed by the terror they had inspired. They realized that they would be harshly dealt with if their secret was disclosed. So, again working under the cover of darkness, they removed the monster from the lake and hid it in the attic of the Walker House.

By the time fire revealed the hoax, the scare had died away and there was no prosecution.

So the Sea Serpent of Silver Lake passed into the folklore of the Genesee Country, another great hoax like the Cardiff Giant of Central New York.

Chapter 9

Canal Days

Seventy-seven years have gone since a boatman's horn echoed through the Deep Cut; since a hoof pounded narrow towpath high above the foaming falls of Portage; since a sharp-nosed packet boat took on passengers at York Landing.

Long ago the Genesee Valley Canal was written off the state ledgers in a welter of red ink. Twenty years and six million dollars had gone into its construction. Engineering, financial and political difficulties had beset it from the beginning. It is a wonder it ever was completed at all. And no sooner was it done all the way from Rochester to Olean than the demand rose for its abandonment.

Yet it was born of a grand dream of the pioneers and it served in its time. Now it is another footnote in local history. Few are left who remember the days when boats plied its slow waters.

Still there are tangible reminders of the old canal in this age of the jet. They are the stone locks in the rocky hills along the road from Nunda to Portageville.

As staunch today as when they were laid, by hand and stone by stone, more than a century ago, those walls are a monument to the determination and stamina of a pioneering generation.

95

For the rock had to be blasted out by hand drills and black powder. There were no steam shovels, no dump trucks. The earth was removed by horse scrapers and in many places where horses could not be used, the soil and broken rock were carried away in the leather aprons of the workmen. A state historical marker stands beside the Deep Cut of the old canal.

The Genesee Valley Canal was hatched in 1825, the year that saw the completion of the Erie Canal across the northern reaches of New York State. It was born of the desperate need of the wheat-growing Genesee Valley and of the lumber-rich Southern Tier for a road to market.

It was the era of the waterways—before the advent of the railroads. The Genesee River was too narrow, too shallow and dotted with too many towering waterfalls to be navigable.

The Erie Canal was too far away to be of great benefit to the Valley or the Tier. Yet it was the success of that "Clinton Ditch" which inspired the promoters of a canal to link the Erie Canal with the Allegheny River.

On June 15, 1825, a call was issued in the Livingston Register for a public meeting "of the citizens of Monroe, Livingston, Allegany, Cattaraugus and Steuben Counties who feel interested in the formation of a canal from Rochester along the Valley of the Genesee and the Canaseraga and of a canal from the Genesee River to some point of the Allegheny River."

The meeting, at the house of Col. John Pierce of Geneseo, "was for the purpose of devising means to collect and convey to the Canal Commissioners and the state government the necessary information as to the practicability and vast importance of the above canal route."

Signers of the call were some of the leading men of the region, including Judge Philip Church, the Allegany County land baron; Daniel Fitzhugh of the Valley landed gentry, and Jonathan Child, destined to be first mayor of Rochester.

In the background was a grandiose plan, often revived since, of widening and improving the Allegheny so that shipments might be made via the Erie and Valley Canals and the Allegheny, Ohio and Mississippi Rivers from northern points to the Gulf of Mexico.

The canal movement was pushed vigorously. A committee was named and several meetings held. But in 1825 a bill providing for the preliminary surveys of the project was defeated in the Legislature. Its sponsor, an obscure freshman Assemblyman, was a Rochester editor named Thurlow Weed, later to become Whig boss of the state.

Finally the surveys were authorized and begun in 1834. The route was to follow the Genesee from Rochester to Mount Morris, where the canal crossed the river and went through the Cushaqua Valley to a point beyond Nunda. It recrossed the Genesee at Portageville and followed the river to Belfast, thence swinging over great hills to Cuba and to Olean on the Allegheny. The plans included a spur from Mount Morris to Dansville through the valley of the Canaseraga.

From Rochester to Mount Morris the route was generally level. The southern reaches presented formidable engineering difficulties. There were the rocky hills south of Nunda, the high-walled canyon and falls at Portage and the hill country southwest of Belfast to reckon with. A canal, only 124 miles long, needed 112 locks because of the rugged terrain. The ditch was 42 feet wide at the top and 26 feet at the bottom, with a depth of four feet.

Work on the Valley Canal lagged from the onset. In 1837 the first 30 Northern miles were put under contract but it was not until 1840 that the 37-mile stretch from Rochester to Mount Morris was completed. That called for a celebration. When the canal reached any sizeable community, residents held their own fiesta. There was no triumphant parade of boats, no 300-mile-long cannon salute, such as marked the opening of the Erie Canal. It took too long to dig the Valley ditch.

Ports in the Rochester-Mount Morris section included Scottsville, which had already dug its own brief canal from mills on the Oatka to the Genesee; Canawaugus, York Landing, Spencerport which became Fowlerville because there already was a Spencerport on a larger canal; Piffard, Cuylerville, Moscow (Leicester) Landing. Thriving settlements mushroomed where had been only farm land. The old Valley Canal spawned some of those communities.

Construction of the canal eased the unemployment problem during the panic (depression in modern lingo) of 1837. Many of the sweating men who actually dug the ditch were just off the boat from Ireland.

Ironically 1837 also was the year that the first steam train puffed out of Rochester for Batavia. The mightiest enemy of the canals had arrived on the scene.

In 1841 four miles of the canal proper from Mount Morris to Shakers Crossing and 11 miles of the Dansville branch had been completed.

Then in 1842 a Democratic state administration came into power and the "Stop Act" halted all construction of the canal for five years.

Meanwhile Elisha Johnson, early railroad builder, engineer-promoter and one time mayor of Rochester, had taken the contract for the building of the Portage section of the canal. He evolved a bold engineering scheme—to carry the canal around the falls of Portage by boring a short-cut tunnel 1,100 feet long, 20 feet wide and 20 feet deep, through the rocky mountain wall above the Genesee gorge.

Above the boring he built a curious residence which he called Hornby Lodge. It was of logs, four stories high and it had 18 rooms. The central room was octagonal. The ceiling was supported by the trunk of a massive oak with the bark left on it. The carpet was fitted four square to the four sides of the sylvan pillar's base.

In his cliff-side abode, Johnson entertained the canal commissioners and other bigwigs in royal style. Sometimes there were 50 guests for dinner. There Johnson's daughter was maried in an elaborate ceremony. There Thomas Cole, the artist, stayed while he was painting the picture of the falls and the canyon that was to grace Governor Seward's Auburn mansion.

Nature wrote its own "Stop Act" to Elisha Johnson's audacious tunnel scheme. After only 300 feet had been dug, continual rock slides forced abandonment of the project. Hornby Lodge was torn down and Johnson soon left for new ventures in Tennessee.

There is a hole in the rocky hillside along the Pennsylvania tracks on the east side of the river just west of the old Civil War parade grounds in Letchworth Park. It is the opening to Elisha Johnson's old tunnel.

Nowadays it is known as "The Bat Cave" because its gloomy interior is the home of more than 4,000 bats. Scientists have found in the cavern all six species of the winged creatures known to exist on the continent. It is said to be the largest bat colony in America. The State Museum and

Science Service seeks to learn more about the mysterious migrating habits of bats and their hibernation habits. About 1,500 bats were banded in 1954 and some turned up in Canada and the deep South.

But too many people other than scientists have been prowling around the "Bat Cave" recently. Fearing more of the rock falls which doomed the Johnson tunnel, authorities are taking steps to seal the cavern to the public. The cave is on the slender right of way of the Pennsylvania although bordered by state park land and the railroad must acquiesce in the building of an iron gate at the entrance. This gate would be locked and only authorized persons (students of the ways of bats) would have keys.

Thus after more than a century the spotlight has swung again on the hole in the hillside that is the symbol of an engineering defeat which cost the state a quarter of a million dollars.

But the engineers really triumphed in pinning the canal to the cliffside, 150 feet above the river, with a narrow towpath winding under the famous Erie High Bridge. The canal crossed the Genesee via a wooden aqueduct on stone piers. Stage service was maintained at the Portage stretch for the benefit of timid passengers.

After the conquest of Portage, the canal builders pushed on through the level river valley, past Portageville, Rossburg, Fillmore, Houghton and Caneadea to reach Oramel in 1851. There 15 million feet of lumber and great piles of staves and shingles were on the banks waiting shipment. Oramel, now a dwindling hamlet, was a bustling port in canal days and Houghton, now the seat of a staid Wesleyan college, was a wild and roaring place called Jockey Street.

In 1853 the ditch reached Belfast. Three years later the

27 miles over the rugged Allegany hills to Olean Basin were dug. In 1857 an additional six and one-half mile stretch from Olean to Mill Grove and the slack water of the Allegheny River was authorized.

There were many problems after the 20-year task of construction was done. One was maintaining a water-tight canal through a hilly, gravelly upland. Another was finding sufficient water to fill and operate the canal.

Neither was fully solved ever. In 1858 the state constructed the largest artificial lake in the world near Cuba. It covered 500 acres and helped to provide the water the ditch needed. Cuba Lake still sparkles in the hills, 1,665 feet above sea level, and lined with summer homes, another lasting reminder of the canal that once ran through five counties from Rochester to Olean.

Rochester millers, dependent on the water power of the Genesee, often complained that the Valley Canal was taking too much river water. But that same ditch up until the 1850s brought from the Genesee Valley, then the vaunted "Breadbox of the Nation," most of the wheat milled in the great, gray stone structures beside the river falls of Rochester, "the Flour City," milling center of the land.

The Valley was in those days the premier wheat-growing region and the Genesee label on a sack of flour was the proudest in the markets.

In the early 1850s the weevil or wheat midge struck the waving golden fields and destroyed the Valley's supremacy as the granary of the East.

Despite the heavy shipments of wheat from the Valley and of lumber and dairy products from the Southern Tier, the canal never fulfilled the expectations of its builders.

The competition of the railroads was too rugged for the

slow-moving canal boats. The contemplated improvement of the Allegheny never materialized. The waterway fell into disrepair, disuse and disfavor and in September of 1878 the state officially abandoned the Genesee Valley Canal. It went the way—and in the same decade—of the Crooked Lake, the Chemung, the Chenango and other lateral canals.

In 1880 the state sold to the Genesee Valley Canal Railroad for $11,400 the right of way of the canal it had cost six million dollars and 20 years to build. The new rail line soon became a part of the Pennsylvania system which still operates it. But now only freight trains—and diesel-drawn ones at that—cover the old route that once knew the packet boats and the barges and in a later time the long red excursion trains taking thousands to the falls of Portage.

The Valley Canal, it is true, wound up as an economic failure. Still in its time it had brought considerable prosperity to an isolated area and it had spawned many a community on its banks.

And on the credit side of the ledger there must be written the intangible things, the life and color that the old ditch brought to the ports it touched.

Picturesque characters navigated the Genesee Valley Canal. One was big, tough Ben Streeter, "The Bully of Rochester," a celebrated rough and tumble fighter. He lived at the Rapids, opposite the present University of Rochester campus and he steered the first boat that ran from Rochester to Mount Morris.

An old canal captain, H. P. Marsh, in 1914 published a rare little paper-covered booklet, *Rochester and Its Early Canal Days.* It contains an account of Ben's fight with "The Bully of Buffalo" in the old Reynolds Arcade. While a crowd

Grand Canyon of the Genesee

Thunder Water—Letchworth Park's Middle Falls

from both cities watched and cheered, "they fought for an hour and Ben licked him; no officer dared interfere."

Captain Marsh wrote of the rivalry between a horse-drawn stage line and the canal packet Frances running between Portageville and Oramel. It was so fierce at one time that each line carried passengers free and the canal boat threw in dinner gratis. The packet boat gave up the ruinous competition. The stage ran until the Pennsylvania Railroad came.

Among the other packets were the Betsy King, the Diantha Mariah, the Nelson Lareau, the Diamond, the May Fly, the Mayflower and the Dansville.

The packet boats were narrow and sharp-prowed. The freight barges had round bows and square sterns. Some were 14 feet wide and 80 feet long and capable of hauling 90 tons of lumber.

In the early days three-horse tandem teams in smart harness trimmings hauled the passenger boats at a trot that averaged four miles an hour, about the pace of a carriage horse on a highway. The deck made an excellent promenade, especially on moonlight nights.

Passengers slept in hammock-like berths which may have given George M. Pullman some of his ideas. They were called sacking frames and made of canvas, hanging on irons fastened to the side of the boat. The steward put them up at bedtime and took them down in the morning to make way for breakfast service.

The arrival of a packet boat was an event in the ports, especially the smaller ones. The sound of the boatman's horn in the distance would bring a crowd down to the dock.

Many of the crews lived on the boats all winter during the off season. The captains who owned their own boats and lived in the region were careful in selecting their crews. The hired captains of the line boats owned by outside companies commanded some rough canalers.

There were saloons all along the line, generally at the locks. There were cut tow lines and fights and often a splash as a luckless crewman was tossed into the shallow, narrow ditch.

And once there was a pitched battle. It was in the canal town of Dansville and the year was 1844. In 1842 a spur of the canal had been completed from Mount Morris to Dansville. The westside of the village along Jefferson Street where the canal terminated became a flourishing center of business.

Main Street merchants viewed this development with dismay. Led by George Hyland and Merritt Brown, they raised $6,000 to dig a slip from the canal terminal to the main business district—without state sanction.

When the time came to cut through the canal bank and let the water into the new spur, the state sent three scowloads of fighting men to Dansville to prevent it. Hyland and Brown met them with their Main Streeters, armed with pickaxes and spades.

A short but fierce battle ensued. The scow gangs were put to flight. The Main Streeters were masters of the field and they cut through the bank without interference. The water rushed toward Main Street.

Some 30 leading citizens were indicted for illegally tapping the state's canal and for resisting the authorities but their cases never came to trial. The new branch and its basin preserved the old center of business. The road along the canal where the Main Streeters won their engagement against the forces of the Empire State was named Battle Street.

In the 1920s a village board that was not historically minded changed the name to Booth Avenue in honor of a family living on the street. In 1951 the *Dansville Breeze* waged a brief but winning editorial campaign to have the name changed back to Battle Street.

The name of a street, a few scattered state markers, a "Bat Cave" in the side of a rocky canyon, some sturdy old stone locks, a radiant lake in the hills, a few pages in local histories—only these remain to tell of the colorful years when the lazy canal water carried the packets and the barges through the Valley of the Genesee.

Chapter 10

Grand Canyon and Thunder Water

There is a Cinderella chapter to the story of the Genesee.

Genesee means in the Indian language "pleasant banks." For 150 miles of the river's meandering, the name fits. Its banks are surely pleasant but they are not spectacular.

But there are 17 other miles so magnificent that the white man has called that segment of the old Indian valley "the Grand Canyon of the East."

There at the place of falling waters known to the Senecas as Portage, the carrying place for the war canoes, Nature touches the river with a magic wand and like Cinderella at the stroke of midnight it throws off its commonplace garb and dons robes of dazzling splendor.

There the patient, implacable river bit by bit through the centuries waged a war of attrition against the massive Devonian rock until it etched the deep chasm through it— the majestic towering walls of mingled gray and green through which the Genesee winds serenely after tumbling grandly over three waterfalls.

The Indians felt in their bones the matchless beauty of the scene and they wove songs and legends about the "three falls of the Jungies."

Today that scenic wonderland is the showplace of the Genesee Country, the 13,300-acre Letchworth State Park.

On a boulder at Inspiration Point, the 375 foot high bluff that commands a superb view of two waterfalls and miles of rock-walled gorge, is this inscription:

> *"God wrought for us this scene beyond compare,*
> *But one man's loving hand protected it*
> *And gave it to his fellow men to share."*

That "one man" was a successful industrialist, reared in the Quaker faith, a gentle, rather shy bachelor of cultivated tastes and with a heart that beat for his fellow men. Letchworth was his name—William Pryor Letchworth—and the extent of his service to his state has never been fully appreciated. Probably that is because he did his good deeds with so little fanfare.

For half a century 1,000 acres of the present park, including the three cataracts, was his private estate. He named it Glen Iris because of the rainbow-hued spray that rose from the Middle Falls in the glen below his mansion.

During his lifetime he protected Glen Iris against interests that coveted the power that lay in its tumbling waters. And in 1907, when a power dam project threatened the natural beauty of the present park, he deeded his magnificent estate to the people of the State of New York. He reserved the use of it during his lifetime. In three years he was dead.

It was a princely gift. The people, not only of New York but of many other states who have come to know the scenic glories of Letchworth Park, are eternally in his debt.

The name of Letchworth should also be revered because of his unselfish service to the unfortunate, particularly the aged, the mentally ill and the epileptic, the forgotten people of his time. For 23 years he served on the State Board of Charities without pay. He visited institutions abroad and brought home new ideas for psychiatric treatment. He fathered the second hospital for epileptics in America, Craig Colony in the Genesee Valley.

It is fitting that the park he gave to posterity should bear his name. It also is fitting that the institution for mental defectives in Rockland County should be called Letchworth Village.

The master of Glen Iris had an absorbing interest in regional history. Because of him there stands on the Council House grounds in the state park such historical treasures as the old Seneca Council House, the statue of Mary Jemison and the log cabin she built. Letchworth made possible the museum in the park, full of relics of Indian and pioneer days.

The 48 years since Glen Iris was given to the state have brought great expansion to Letchworth Park. As we shall see that has been largely due to various plans for harnessing the waters of the Genesee in the river gorge.

The state park of nearly 13,300 acres stretching for 17 miles along the grand canyon, which at one point towers 550 feet above the river bed, contains the three mighty cataracts—the Upper Falls, 71 feet high, its waters tossing under the 235 foot Portage High Bridge of the Erie Railroad, a familiar landmark in the Valley—the Middle Falls whose waters tumble down a 107 foot ledge—the Lower Falls, 70 feet high where the Genesee narrows to eight feet at one point, the place of the foot bridge and the Cathedral Rock.

Also in this park of woodland trails, scenic parkways and a vast arboretum are:

The flats of Gardeau where lived Mary Jemison, the White Woman of the Genesee; the sites of two once lively villages, St. Helena and Gibsonville, now vanished from the scene;

109

a parade and drill ground of the Civil War where Union recruits from the region were taught their first lessons in the art of war. Once upon a time there stretched above the Upper Falls the largest and highest wooden bridge in the world.

It is estimated that in this year of 1955 the state park will have a total of a half million visitors. They come from far places. In a 15-minute check of parking places I counted the license plates of cars from 18 states and Canada.

Letchworth Park is only 55 miles from Rochester. Yet there are Rochesterians who have never seen the scenic wonderland that is at their very door. Some of them don't have any idea where the park is.

But then I have heard of Buffalo people who lived and died without ever seeing Niagara Falls.

*   *   *

The geologic story of the grand canyon is written in the rocks for the scientist to read. One scientist, the foremost geologist of the Genesee Country, the late Dr. Herman Leroy Fairchild of the University of Rochester, recorded the story and this is its gist:

The exposed rocks in the gorge are shales and sandstones formed during the Devonian period when the Valley lay under shallow seas. Then many centuries ago the Genesee carved out a broad valley through the soft rocks. North of Portageville the course of the ancient river lay east of the present park.

In the glacial time the great ice sheet moved down from the North and buried this region under tons of ice thousands of feet deep. The glaciers brought great masses of rock which were deposited in an irregular pattern in the valleys. One of the heaviest of these deposits was in the present park and it filled the old river valley.

In time the glaciers retreated and a series of lakes was formed. One of them south of the park, barred from the old path of the Genesee by glacial masses, found an outlet to the north and formed the canyon in the southerly section of the park. This led to a second lake in the central area near the site of St. Helena. Later by the same process the northerly part of the gorge was created, leading into the original Valley.

Of course all that took place countless years ago. During the post-glacial centuries the river by slow and steady erosion carved out the present grand canyon.

The first man to see the crowning glory of the Genesee Country may have been Etienne Brule, courier for Champlain, the governor of New France, on his long trek from the land of the Hurons to the capital of the Andaste nation near the present Waverly, N. Y. in 1615. While Brule left no records, his logical course would have been through the Genesee Country.

There is no question about the first white woman to marvel at the grandeur of the gorge and waterfalls. She was Mary Jemison who first came to the Valley in 1762 and who lived most of her long life a few miles from the thunder water.

While the Indians were filled with awe at the majesty of the three falls, they must also have regarded the cataracts as something of a nuisance. For the falls were a barrier to navigation of the river and the Senecas had to carry their canoes around them. The old Indian portage trail, later used by the white settlers, today is one of the park's scenic parkways.

White settlement began in the area as early as 1809 in what

111

is now the town of Castile. Much of the land was in the Cotringer tract which was put on the market in 1816.

There sprang up on the river south of the Upper Falls a settlement first called Schuyler after Philip Schuyler of Revolutionary fame. Later it became Portage and finally Portageville.

Lumbering was the principal occupation in the early days. The steep hills were thickly covered with oak, chestnut and pine. Logs were floated on the river to a saw mill at Portageville and the sawed lumber was drawn down the "Carrying Road," the old Indian portage, during the Winter, ready to be rafted on the river in the Spring.

The carrying road was little used after the coming of the Genesee Valley Canal. Work was begun on the canal in the area in 1837. It was suspended after three years and resumed in 1849. The building of the aqueduct and of the ill-fated tunnel, a canal short-cut that was abandoned, provided plenty of work and Portageville was a lively place.

The boom was accelerated in 1850 when work began on the Portage High Bridge of the Attica & Hornellsville Railway, which later became and still is a part of the Erie system.

Bridging the mighty gorge of the Genesee presented a problem to the railroad builders. The engineers answered the challenge with the largest wooden bridge in the world. Portage Bridge was 800 feet long and 234 feet high.

It crossed the chasm directly over the foaming Upper Falls. For 78 years the High Bridge and the falls below it have been the target of the picture takers. Hundreds of thousands of pictures have been snapped of the scene. Many camera fans have waited hours for a train to crawl over the High Bridge.

Two years went into assembling the material for the span

before a rail was laid. Into the structure went 1,600,000 linear feet of lumber, the product of nearly 300 acres of standing pine. The timbers, as well as 106,000 pounds of iron for the bridge, came by canal boat and highway wagon.

Construction of the $175,000 bridge fascinated the engineering world of the mid 19th Century and not only because of its size. It was so fabricated that if any unit proved defective that unit could be removed and replaced without disturbing the rest of the structure.

The building of the railroad in the Portage section brought a management-labor clash which caused a lot of excitement in 1851 and has its place in history as "The Portage Riot."

Here is the hardly objective account of the affray as told by Livingston L. Doty in his *History of Livington County:*

"A large number of the laborers on the section of the New York and Erie Railroad running through Portage, struck for higher wages and as is generally the case, not only refused to work themselves but would not permit others to do so. So annoying were the strikers in their efforts to prevent others from working that a requisition was made on the civil authorities of Livingston and Wyoming Counties.

"A half dozen officers repaired to the scene. A desperate encounter ensued between the officers and the disaffected workers in which a number of the latter were shot, two at least fatally. Then a requisition was made to Captain Hamilton at Geneseo for the services of the Big Tree Artillery and that organization started for the scene of conflict. The sight of the militia cowed the rioters and without any serious objection, 20 of their number were arrested. The principal offenders were properly punished."

Historian Doty did not mention that the workmen, mostly

113

Irish emigrants, received only 6½ cents an hour, worked in some cases from 4 A.M. to 7:30 P.M. and had to board themselves on 7 shillings a day.

While the workers lost their strike, they gained some concessions and work on the railroad and the High Bridge went on.

The versatile James Mack of Portageville, rural mail carrier, dealer in antiques and collector of regional relics and lore, who works land his father before him farmed, told me a tale of Yorker ingenuity which he had heard years ago from one of the oldtimers.

Before the wooden bridge was completed, the railroad needed to get a locomotive, one of those old wood burners, from the east to the west side of the Genesee gorge.

The road's best minds were baffled. A reward was offered for the solution of the problem. Two Castile men, who owned a couple of stump pulling machines and had been yanking hundreds of stumps out of the countryside, came up with a plan.

First the water was drained out of the 10-ton locomotive and extra axles put under it. Then it was wheeled down the old carrying road by use of a stump puller, a windlass-like affair with a big wheel attached to a cable hitched to a horse which a boy rode in a circle.

After the bottom of the hill was reached, the locomotive was loaded on the state scow used on the Genesee Valley Canal which took it to the west side river dock. There 20 yoke of oxen hauled it up the road to the west end of the bridge. The Castile stump pullers had won the prize, solved the problem that had stumped the engineers. Jim Mack did not know the exact amount of the reward but it was a substantial sum.

Finally the big wooden bridge was completed and in August, 1852, the first train, with four coaches filled with notables, rumbled over it. But not until a mammoth celebration had been held. United States Senator William H. Seward and Governor Washington Hunt who had lived as a boy at nearby Hunt's Hollow, spoke. Bands played and cannons thundered. Roast ox was served to thousands and, according to accounts of the celebration, "the meat somehow caused a cholera" which made many ill.

The towering bridge above the waterfalls, an engineering marvel of the time, became a showplace of the region. A shrewd and enterprising veteran of the War of 1812 early saw its possibilities and capitalized on it.

He was Col. George Williams, a nephew of John Greig, one of Canandaigua's leading land owners. Williams had acquired considerable land in and around Portageville. But he visualized the eastern end of the High Bridge as the coming place and acquired large holdings there. He saw that Portageville's star as a boom town had set.

The colonel built a rambling and elegant three-story wooden hotel near the new railroad station which flaunted the sign, "Portage." The Cascade House is still there, a magnificent ruin. Another hotel across the way, a cluster of houses, a store or two were built and Portage was born at the eastern end of the High Bridge. The railroad ran excursions there. Thousands came to marvel at the canyon, the great bridge and the tossing falls. For many years Portage was a lively place and fulfilled the colonel's expectations. Williams built a mansion nearby and until he died in 1876 he was the lord of the manor at Portage.

In the 1860s things really hummed there but the bustle had grim overtones. It was the time of civil war and Portage

115

in 1862 became a training camp for volunteers of the region. It was named Camp Williams after the colonel. A drill ground was laid out on a level field and barracks were hastily built. They proved inadequate and Portage householders took in the overflow of citizen soldiers.

Farmers from the hills, shopkeepers and mechanics from the towns learned the ABCs of war on Portage drill ground. The First Dragoons and the 136th Infantry were among the volunteer outfits mustered in at Camp Williams.

Today the place that once echoed to the bark of military commands and the tramp of marching feet is a sylvan picnic site in Letchworth State Park. Only a boulder tells of its hour of martial glory. Once there was a plaque on the big stone. Park authorities had to remove it for safe keeping. Impish boys kept taking it off.

* * *

Among those who came to look at the wondrous High Bridge of Portage in the 1850s was a young Buffalo manufacturer named William Pryor Letchworth. He was struck with the beauty of the place but appalled by the abandoned saw mill, the lumber, stumps and shavings that littered the high banks of the river. Even then there were those who eyed the latent power of the waterfalls and hoped to establish a manufacturing center in the glen beside the Middle Falls.

In 1859 Letchworth bought 1,000 acres around the three falls for his summer home. According to some accounts he remodeled an old house on the site into the mansion which today is the Glen Iris Inn. Other historians state Letchworth built a brand new home there. Certainly it was a charming

116

residence with stately lines and pillars that graced the western high banks directly above the Middle Falls.

The master of the scenic estate which he called Glen Iris got rid of the saw mill and the clutter. He hollowed out a pool, fed by water brought from hillside springs through a conduit and made a fountain on his grounds.

William Letchworth was only 36 years old when he acquired his estate at Portage. He had come a long way up the ladder in the Horatio Alger tradition—without marrying the boss's daughter. In fact he never married.

He was born of Quaker parents in Brownsville, Jefferson County, in 1823. At the age of 15 he went to Auburn to learn the harness business for $40 a year and his keep. Somehow he managed to save $2 out of his first year's pay. In Auburn he formed a lasting friendship with a rising young politician-lawyer named William Henry Seward, an eagle-beaked, cigar-smoking, fast talking fellow, the antithesis of the quiet Letchworth.

Letchworth left Auburn to enter business in New York. After seven years in the metropolis he moved to Buffalo in 1848 to become a junior partner in the firm of Pratt and Letchworth, makers of saddlery goods and carriage hardware. The business expanded with the booming lake port. A factor was Letchworth's pioneering use of malleable iron.

For 10 years his business was his life. At the age of 35 he had acquired a comfortable fortune. Then he realized that "business had drawn all my attention from literature, knowledge and art." He made a pilgrimage to Europe to cultivate those neglected matters.

Then came his purchase of Glen Iris and a new and gracious way of life for the man of business. He retained his interest in Buffalo civic affairs but turned more to the cultural. He spent all his Summers and many week ends at his country place which he was developing into one of the finest private estates in America.

He planted trees and embellished the grounds. He invited cultivated people to his mansion. There was tea and good talk in his quiet study. David Gray, the Buffalo writer and William C. H. Hosmer, "the Bard of Avon, N. Y." were among his guests, as well as his friend Seward. Letchworth became interested in the affairs of the countryside and in its rich history.

In the 1860s Letchworth also became interested, so the story goes, in a young and handsome pioneer woman physician, Dr. Cornelia A. Greene, who conducted a private sanitarium in the nearby village of Castile. Her father, Jabez, had founded the "water cure" in 1849. It is still operating and still in the hands of the family.

Soon Doctor Greene received the gift of a fine barouche, right from the Pratt and Letchworth showrooms. The distinguished pair were often seen in it together. There were picnic trips to Silver Lake, to Fall Brook and other spots. The country people wagged their heads and their tongues but no engagement was ever announced. William Letchworth and Cornelia Greene remained good friends as long as they lived.

The master of Glen Iris had a sentimental streak in his make-up. Otherwise would he have designed the romantic "Romeo and Juliet" balcony for the second story of his mansion just above the singing falls? It leads to the "bridal suite" at the Inn today.

He was fond of children and entertained wagon loads of them at his estate. Some of them were "fresh air kids" from city streets, others country youngsters. He gave prizes to

118

honor pupils in regional schools and a proud possession of many an aging man and woman is a book with the name, "W. P. Letchworth," written on the flyleaf, a symbol of a scholastic triumph of long ago.

Letchworth had a flair for the graphic phrase. When on the night of May 6, 1875, the massive wooden Erie bridge caught fire and burned, he watched the awesome spectacle and wrote that "the water was glistening with the bright glare thrown upon it and the whole valley of Glen Iris was illuminated with tragic splendor."

Supposedly the High Bridge caught fire from sparks from a wood-burning locomotive crossing it. Natives of the region through the years have thrown a cloak of mystery about that night the great bridge burned, lighting up the sky for miles around, and blazing timbers fell splashing into the Genesee.

You hear tales that have been handed down from father to son—"that it was strange no watchman was on duty the night of the fire—that the whole thing was a mass of flames in a matter of minutes." Mystery or no, it was a most spectacular happening in that valley of the spectacular.

Crews of grim and sweating men, toiling 47 nights and days, replaced the wooden bridge with a wrought iron span, one foot higher than the old one. It was regarded as an engineering feat in 1875. But again in Portageville lore, "it was strange that the railroad was able to find iron already fabricated of the right dimensions, supposedly for a bridge in Africa, thus saving much time." In later years the bridge was reinforced with steel.

Five years before the bridge fire made history, William Pryor Letchworth, whose interest in regional history was quickening, bought a historic building. It was the old Seneca Council House at Caneadea, a log structure which had been

119

built by the British, possibly during the Revolution, for their Indian allies, the gathering place of the savage raiding parties, the scene of council fires, whose walls had echoed to the eloquence of Red Jacket, Cornplanter and Joseph Brant.

After the Senecas sold their Caneadea Reservation in 1826, the old Council House fell into disuse and disrepair. Letchworth had it dismantled with each piece carefully marked. Then it was moved the 15 miles from Caneadea and reassembled on a bluff near his mansion just as carefully and its weak spots reinforced.

Within its walls was to be reenacted one more chapter in the drama of the Genesee. On Oct. 1, 1872 when Glen Iris was ablaze with the colors of the Autumn, a fire flamed for the first time in nearly 50 years in the last Council House of the Seneca Nation.

It was the last council fire on the Genesee and around it gathered the descendants of famous chiefs of the Senecas and the Mohawks, the greatest powers of the Iroquois Confederacy.

The meeting healed an old rift between the Mohawks who had gone into Canadian exile under Brant after the Revolution and who had fought with the British in the War of 1812, and the Senecas, who had remained in New York and espoused the American cause in the second war with England.

From Canada came Capt. W. J. Simcoe Kerr, grandson of Brant, wearing that Mohawk chieftain's tomahawk in his belt, to smoke the pipe of peace with the descendants of Red Jacket, Cornplanter and other Seneca chiefs and of Mary Jemison. All were in full ceremonial regalia.

They sat on rustic benches around the fire. In the old

120

days they would have squatted on the floor. A comfortable chair was provided for an aging and distinguished guest, Millard Fillmore of Buffalo, a former President of the United States, who during the ceremonies presented a medal to each Indian.

Again the old Council House resounded to the sonorous oratory of a race of orators. One of the speakers was Nicholas Parker, a grandnephew of Red Jacket. After smoking the tomahawk pipe that had belonged to his silver-tongued ancestor, Parker arose and the shade of Red Jacket must have looked down in approbation as the words rolled out in the orator's apogee:

"Brothers, we are holding council, perhaps for the last time in Gen-nis-heo (Genesee). Brothers, we came here to perform a ceremony but I cannot make it such. My heart says this is not a play or a pageant. It is solemn reality to me and not a mockery of days that are past and can never return. Neh-hoh—this is all."

"Neh-hoh"—the audience repeated the closing word. It was as the chanting of a requiem for the last glory of a once mighty people. Other speakers, brave in plumes, beaded sashes and belts, followed Parker. Cornplanter's grandson, old Solomon O'Bail, extended the hand of fellowship to Colonel Kerr, grandson of the Mohawk Brant and tears stood in the eyes of both men, members of a race trained never to show emotion.

Seneca John Jacket, grandson of Red Jacket, the Demosthenes of the Keepers of the Western Door, planted a tree near the west door of the Council House, and Mohawk Kate Osborne, granddaughter of Brant, leader of the guardians of the Long House's Eastern gate, planted another near the eastern door.

121

There was another ceremony that day. This one was held on the lawn of the Letchworth residence and the Indians in their gay costumes moved in their stately dances and chanted their ceremonial songs as William Letchworth was made a member of the Wolf Clan and given the name of Hai-wa-ye-is-tah, "the man who does the right thing."

The old Council House is one of the historical treasures of the state park. The crevices between the foot-thick logs, dovetailed together, are chinked with cement. In the center of its roof of large split shingles is a smoke vent in lieu of a chimney. Still standing at one end of the building are the three great stones taken from the bed of the Genesee to make the hearth for the stone fireplace. There are bars across the paneless windows. The doors are never opened save by a caretaker.

On the log wall of its interior are carved a rude symbol of the Cross and the sacred totem of the Snipe Clan. There are other carvings on its exterior—the initials of sweethearts and swains who have visited the Council House during the past 83 years.

In 1874 Letchworth had the bones of Mary Jemison brought from the Seneca burying ground on Buffalo Creek and reinterred near the Council House. He had the bronze statue placed above her grave and the log house she built brought from Gardeau. The Council House Grounds at Letchworth Park will always be a shrine of Genesee history, thanks to "the man who does the right thing."

Letchworth retired from business in 1873 and Glen Iris became his all-season home. Then began a new phase of his immensely useful career. He possessed no great fortune as we know riches today but he had enough to help his fellow men the rest of his days.

In 1873, the year of his retirement, he was appointed a member of the state board of charities. He entered on his duties with conscientious zeal. He visited poor houses throughout the state and what he saw appalled him. He found young pauper children housed with the aged, the senile, the depraved, the insane.

He studied the care of the unfortunate in institutions all over the country and in 1880 made a trip to Europe at his own expense. In orphanages and reformatories abroad he discovered vocational therapy, the honor system, playgrounds instead of high walls, the cottage plan of putting children in groups under a house father and other advanced methods. He came home to urge their adoption in his own state.

He studied the institutions for the care of the mentally ill in Europe and returned to advocate broader and more sympathetic understanding of mental disease, more attractive and home-like environments, healthful employment and recreation, better doctors and nurses.

These ideas were considered revolutionary in a state whose mentally ill were housed generally in almshouses, along with the diseased and the indigent, where pauper, wayward and orphaned children were confined behind stone walls as if they were desperate criminals.

His crusade led along no easy road. State legislators were loath to make any changes that would spell appropriations and tax increases. But Letchworth was a patient and persevering man. He published his European findings in pamphlets and slowly his ideas gained ground. Eventually pauper children were placed in separate institutions and in foster homes. The state, not individual counties, was given exclusive care of the mentally ill. Separate state asylums for the insane were established.

Letchworth was largely responsible for closing the medieval walled-in House of Refuge in Rochester and supplanting it with the State School for boys at Industry on rolling country acres.

After 23 years as a member of the state charities body, nine of them as its president, Letchworth resigned in 1896. But his work for the afflicted was by no means done.

He began a crusade for that pariah among the diseased, the epileptic. Those unfortunates were housed in almshouses and asylums and virtually nothing was done for them.

Letchworth helped push a bill through the Legislature providing for a state hospital for epileptics. He was instrumental in picking its location, the site of an old Seneca village named Sonyea which means "sunny place." Sonyea is in the town of Groveland, southeast of Mount Morris. He suggested that it be given the name of Craig Colony, in honor of Oscar Craig of Rochester, a member of the state charities commission.

The state in 1894 purchased 1,800 acres and 30 buildings from the United Society of Christian Believers, commonly known as the Shakers, because of the twitching of their bodies under the spell of religious frenzy.

The Shakers, thrifty, law-abiding, hard-working folk, who wore the plainest of clothes and were followers of the doctrines of Mother Ann Lee of Lebanon, had established a colony at Sodus Bay in 1823. Thirteen years later they sold their tract at a profit when a ship canal was projected—but never dug—from Sodus Bay to Clyde.

Then "the Plain People" bought the tract at Sonyea from Daniel Fitzhugh of the valley gentry. They erected some imposing buildings, including the House of the Elders, a four-story dormitory, a central meeting house, a chapel, a flour mill, a saw mill, a broom shop, fruit houses, barns and a laundry.

They were good farmers. They harvested straw for the making of brooms and sold garden seeds, as well as garden produce. Oldtimers in the Valley remember the Shakers in their sober garb driving their wagons to market at Mount Morris. A port on the Valley Canal and a railroad crossing were called Shakers. But both the Canal and railroad are defunct now.

But their practice of celibacy restricted their numbers and they leaped at the chance to sell their holdings to the state for $115,000. They had been plagued by fires and some dishonest trustees had eloped with community funds. In January, 1896, the first patient was admitted to Craig Colony. The four-story brick dormitory was remodeled for the use of patients and renamed Letchworth House, a name it still bears. At least five other buildings at Craig Colony today were built by the Shakers. The House of the Elders was razed in 1947 after it had been ruined by fire. In one corner of Craig Colony is the old Shaker burying ground.

As long as he lived, Letchworth helped guide the destinies of the colony of which he was the real father. Craig Colony, the only institution in the state exclusively for the care of epileptics and the second one established in the nation, today has more than 2,300 patients, one half of whom live in cottages and have freedom of the grounds. The colony has more than 700 employees. Its payroll is not insignificant in the Valley economy.

In 1898 the master of Glen Iris provided the funds for a museum near his home for the housing of historical relics of the Genesee region. The present stone museum was erected by the American Scenic and Historic Preservation Society after his death.

The simple, gracious style of living at Glen Iris was ever the same. Distinguished visitors received the same treatment as the farm folk and the villagers. The quiet-spoken, spare, kindly gentleman with the gray chin whiskers was well loved, especially by his employees.

In his struggling youth, Quaker-bred William Pryor Letchworth had evolved for himself these "Rules of Conduct":

"Rise at 6 o'clock. Breakfast at 6:30. Dinner or lunch at 12:30. Supper at 6:30. Retire at 9:30. Attend Divine service once every Sunday. Tell the truth under all circumstances . . . Never wound the feelings of others if it can be avoided. Strive always to be cheerful. Review the actions of the day every night and apply to them the test of my conscience. In business affairs keep in mind that 'procrascination is the thief of time' and that 'time is money.' Be temperate in all things.

"Strive to speak kindly without giving offense, always with coolness and deliberation and having due regard for the views of others. Aim at a high standard of character. Attempt great things and expect great things. Aim to do all possible good in the world and so live as to live hereafter and to have a name without reproach."

It was a pretty large order but all his life he lived up to his code—even to the hours of rising and retiring.

In 1903 he suffered a stroke and after that most of his days were in a wheel chair. That was the year the staff and patients of Craig Colony gave him a loving cup. No patient was allowed to give more than five cents. There were many rare art objects, some of them from abroad, surrounding him in his mansion but none was so prized as that little cup.

In his last years Letchworth devoted much thought to the preservation for all the people of the scenic glory of Glen Iris. He consulted with officials of the American Scenic and Historic Preservation Society which had saved the Palisades of the Hudson and Watkins Glen from exploitation. He wanted that group to have control and management of his estate after he was gone.

In 1906 the natural beauty of Glen Iris was gravely menaced. The Genesee River Company, armed with a broad grant to divert water from the three falls of Portage, planned a power dam near Portageville.

The old man in the wheel chair acted swiftly. He offered the State of New York his magnificent estate as a public park, reserving the right of its use during his lifetime.

There was no written agreement, no public announcement of a deal between Letchworth and the State, but there is little doubt that the gift was made contingent on the demise of the power dam project. And in due time the State of New York denied an application for the construction of a power dam south of the present park.

On Jan. 14, 1907 Governor Charles E. Hughes signed the bill accepting Glen Iris for the state. The Governor later visited Letchworth to thank the donor in person. Under the terms of the gift, the property was to be under the jurisdiction of the Preservation Society. Later that body ceded control to the State Park Commission.

When on Sept. 19, 1910, the statue of Mary Jemison, one of Letchworth's prized projects, was dedicated, the old man was too weak to attend the ceremony.

On Dec. 1 of that year William Pryor Letchworth departed this life. His gentle spirit will always hover over the Glen of the Iris in the grand canyon of the Genesee.

*   *   *

During Letchworth's lifetime the gates of Glen Iris were never closed. The philanthropist was eager to share the scenic wonders of his estate with the public. But from the end of the Civil War to the flowering of the Automotive Age in the 20th Century, Portage, at the east end of the High Bridge, was the mecca of the crowds.

The Erie ran excursion trains from Buffalo and from Hornell, Elmira and other southern points. Near Portage Station were two popular hotels, the big and elegant Cascade House and the Portage House (once the Emerald Hotel) across the way. Both are deserted and rotting away today. But in Portage's heyday they were lively places, especially their bar rooms. There were dances in the third-floor ballroom of the Cascade House and if one tired of wining, dining and dancing, there were the splendors of nature and the High Bridge, in itself a marvel of engineering, to be seen and admired.

Portgage was a Williams principality and George, son of the old colonel, and after him, a son-in-law named Edwin Patterson, operated the Cascade House until its days of glory were over.

The Pennsylvania, operating in the abandoned bed of the old canal, and with its station in the village of Portageville, also went after the excursion trade. Long red trains rolled out of Rochester's Pennsy station on West Main Street and from Olean at the southern end of the line.

In yellowing files of *The Rochester Democrat and Chronicle* under date of 1903, I ran across this ad of the Pennsylvania Railroad:

128

"Fifty cents round trip to romantic Portage Falls. Special train leaves Rochester Sunday at 9:30 A.M., leaves Portage Station at 4:45 P.M."

A horse-drawn stage shuttled between the depots at Portage and at Portageville, meeting all trains. Now neither railroad carries passengers and only freights rumble over the High Bridge or follow the course of the Genesee Valley Canal.

In excursion days Portageville had two hotels, the Bristol, near the station and the Genesee Falls, also known as the Joyce House. The Bristol has been long gone but the three-story Genesee Falls Hotel of warm red brick and roomy porches beside the rock-bottomed river still maintains its century-old tradition of good cheer, good food and good lodging. No village has a finer inn than this one at the southern gate of Letchworth Park.

For years Portage was the rendezvous for the veterans of the conflict which they always called "the War of the Rebellion." They "rallied around the flag" at their old camp ground and they "shouted the battle cry of freedom" in the bars of Portage. The annual reunions of the First Dragoons, recruited from the immediate region, were held at the site of their first wartime camp.

In 1903 a tall monument was erected on a hill near the parade grounds in honor of the Dragoons. There the veterans flocked for patriotic gatherings and reunions. But the blue ranks grew thinner with the years and around the time of World War I, it was voted to move the monument to Letchworth Park. By then Portage's star had set.

Moving the massive column was, if you will pardon the pun, a monumental job. The two parts, the base and shaft, were loaded on railroad flat cars which took them across the

High Bridge. Then teams and wagons hauled the Civil War monument to its present site in the state park.

Now Portage at the end of the High Bridge is almost a ghost town. The Erie station, once such a busy place, has been torn down. Spiders weave their webs in the abandoned hotels. But the Cascade House retains its air of magnificence even in decay. And the lilacs bloom around its doors every Springtime as they did when crowds stood on its balconies. There are a few houses along the old road that leads to Portageville. Some of them housed the soldiers in the Civil War. Silence reigns at Portage where once swelled the merry voices of the excursionists and the fifes and drums of the Grand Army of the Republic.

* * *

From the beginning the development of Letchworth State Park has been closely linked to various proposals for dams and reservoirs in the gorge of the Genesee.

We have seen how in 1907 W. P. Letchworth gave his 1,000 acre estate to the state to preserve his treasured waterfalls from being despoiled by a proposed power dam.

When in the middle 1920s the Rochester Gas and Electric Corporation planned a power dam in the canyon near Mount Morris, the state began buying additional land to protect the scenic areas and also accepted from the utility excess lands on the edge of the proposed reservoir area. By these measures the original 1,000 acres of the park were expanded to some 6,700 acres by 1930. The Rochester company gave up the dam idea with the development of steam power production, which proved more economical than hydro power.

The Genesee, normally a sober, well-behaved stream, through the years has been wont to go on sprees in the

Springtime when the snows melt, the ice breaks up and the rains come. At irregular intervals since white settlement a dozen major floods have struck the Valley. The greatest was on St. Patrick's Day of 1865 which converted the Valley into one vast lake and caused one million dollars damage in Rochester alone.

As early as 1889 the state studied the possibility of a flood control reservoir in the gorge. However the primary aim was to provide a water storage for the Erie Canal. Nothing came of it.

In 1936 the United States authorized a survey of Valley flood control measures. Five years later Federal Engineers proposed a flood control dam south of Mount Morris, at virtually the same spot picked by the power company in the 1920s.

Congress authorized the construction of the Mount Morris dam in 1944. Construction began on the $20,000,000 project on March 22, 1948. The last bucket of concrete was poured on Oct. 31, 1951. At the peak of construction, it had employed 550 workers.

The dam is a concrete structure with lines so graceful that it blends well with its picturesque High Banks background. Its total height from foundation to top of operations tower is 282 feet, making it the fourth highest in the East. It impounds the runoff from a watershed of 1,077 square miles.

With all tributaries of the river running full banks and all hollows of farm land filled with surface water, a five and one half inch rainfall in 24 hours would bring the water up to the top of the spillway. This would put it at the same elevation as the foot of the Lower Falls in the state park. Such a rainfall is not expected but the dam was built for such a contingency.

131

The Mount Morris Dam has already proved its worth. Since its completion Valley residents, particularly those living just south of Rochester, have not had to flee their homes in rowboats as in earlier years. Flood damage has been kept at a minimum on the Genesee flats, too.

The dam, which has given the nearby namesake village of Mount Morris a picturesque slogan, "Best Town by a Dam Site," was built strictly as a flood control project. However it includes two 19 foot penstocks and could be converted into a power dam.

Sightseers in the Grand Canyon of the East may view the big dam from an overlook leading off a state parkway and thousands of them do. The federal dam not only has provided an additional spectacle. It also brought about a considerable expansion of the park acreage.

At the time the federal project was proposed, the state added some 7,000 acres in accordance with its policy of protecting the scenic areas. Now the United States has turned over for the state park's use the 3,300 acres it bought from the Rochester power company around the dam. The power company transferred 300 wooded acres to the state park in 1954. Other smaller parcels have been acquired until today Letchworth's 1,000 acre Glen Iris has grown to a state recreational reserve of 13,261 acres—and the end is not yet by any means.

Letchworth Park is under the jurisdiction of the Genesee State Park Commission, of which Wolcott J. Humphrey, Warsaw banker, has been chairman for many years. The general manager of the commission, which also controls Hamlin Beach State Park on Lake Ontario, is Gordon W. Harvey.

Harvey came to the Genesee in 1938 as park engineer. He is a veteran of 26 years of park service and received his early

The other man, a well-known lawyer who has a[n] summer home in the neighborhood and has know[n] [re]gion all his life, rattled off facts about the nearest drive-ins and mentioned a nearby motor court-resta[urant] grill that brings big name wrestlers to the countryside [?] where "on Saturday nights six bartenders are kept on t[he] jump."

Then quietly and with a different note in his voice, the older man said:

"And there's a park up there, you know, that is quite a wonderful place."

How right he was! Letchworth State Park is a wonderful place—fully as wonderful as the place where six bartenders are kept on the jump on Saturday nights.

training under Robert Moses, present head of the state parks, in the development of Jones Beach and other Long Island areas.

Gordon Harvey is a dedicated man. He eats, sleeps and talks Letchworth State Park. He has seen the annual number of visitors grow from less than 100,000 in 1938 to 437,000 in 1954. He estimates the park will entertain a half million in 1955. He visualizes an eventual one million visitors a year.

Some of the people come for a few hours. Others come to spend weeks, either at the stately Glen Iris Inn that was Letchworth's home, at the new seven motel cabin units, the 74 rustic cabins scattered throughout the park or as campers.

The record of cabin registration shows that 20 per cent of the occupants come from outside New York State and that 32 per cent of them are from outside Western New York. They come from such far off places as California, Arizona, North Carolina. Many are "repeaters."

The park flaunts its gayest colors in the Autumn and draws its biggest crowds on the Sunday nearest October 12 each year, when the foliage is at its zenith.

Harvey's planning embraces development of the whole vast and varied reaches of the park and to scatter its attractions, for years centered around the Middle Falls.

In the expansion program of the 1950s which included the new and modern administration building near Inspiration Point, the fine swimming pool and bathhouse and the cafeteria were located in the Lower Falls area.

New parkways and cabin and picnic sites (the park has 10) are being developed on the east side of the river and in the northern stretches of the park, which are to be preserved in their natural state. There the river has been stocked with wall-eyed pike.

The park director has ambitious plans for the northern section. He hopes one day to have a swimming pool there. Already plans are being made for extending the park road into the edge of Mount Morris, which would place Letchworth's northern entrance only 34 miles from Rochester. The distance to the southern gateway at Portageville is 55 miles.

The park carries on a continuous reforestration program. Its arboretum contains 400,000 trees. The park has its own saw mill. Letchworth State Park is a king-size enterprise.

It has many sides. There is history in the Council House Grounds and in the Museum, which is full of relics of Indian and pioneer times. Carlos Stebbins' portrait of Mary Jemison, in her Indian garb as the first settlers saw her, looks down from the wall. In cases below are the White Woman's last will and testament, her knife, her chair, wool wheel, yarn wheel, a lock of her hair and various protographs.

There are Indian pipes, pottery, ceremonial stones, hatchets and arrowheads. The pioneer collection includes a wooden awl made by Horatio Jones when he was a captive of the Senecas; an 18th Century candle mold, a drum of the War of 1812, and all manner of early farming tools and household utensils.

And in the Museum is an old, old resident of the Genesee Country, the remains of the 5,000 year old giant-tusked mastodon unearthed in 1876 on a farm beside the Wiscoy in the town of Pike.

A room houses the library of Letchworth and some of the curios he gathered. There are more across the way in the century-old Glen Iris Inn, the gracious white-pillared mansion in its warm coat of yellow, under spreading old trees and above the music of the Middle Falls.

The charm of a bygone time clings to the Inn, [...]aken staircase, its romantic balconies, its high-ce[...] rooms whose windows are centered with glass of r[...] hues surrounding an etching right out of Godey'[...] Book.

In the hall are Swiss cowbells that Letchworth picl[...] in Europe. Over the desk as you register the urbane [...] Fillmore watches and in an adjoining room the ma[...] Glen Iris looks down from the wall.

This is no ordinary inn, perched above the tossing [...] Thousands have crossed its hospitable thresholds and [...] its grace.

The tourists have come to know the scenic highlig[...] the park, the names that are on the maps—Inspiration [...] Great Bend, Wolf Creek, Tea Table, the Knob. But [...] are quiet woodland trails and sylvan nooks that ha[...] name, yet are soothing to the eye and mind. And some[...] from one of those unnamed spots you catch a sudden br[...] taking view of towering canyon wall or the far swee[...] wooded hills.

And there are homey touches that have naught to do [...] spectacular scenery—such as the 13 racoons that Perry [...] son, veteran general park foreman, has tamed so tha[...] nights people go to the lawn of his yellow house near Insp[...] tion Point to feed the shy creatures. Warily the 'coons [...] vance, grab the bit of bread crust you hold out, then ret[...] back into the shadows with gleaming eyes. But they [...] swarm all over Perry Wilson, even sit upon his lap.

One evening in the cozy tap room of the Genesee F[...] Hotel at Portageville, I overheard a tourist, a young n[...] with a Bronx accent, ask an older man at an adjoining tak[...]

"Any excitement around here?"

Chapter 11

The Deserted Villages

Once upon a time—and it wasn't so long ago—there were two lively little communities in the shadow of the High Banks on the west side of the Genesee River.

Their names were Gibsonville and St. Helena and each had its streets, its cluster of houses, mills, stores, a schoolhouse and in those days:

> *"Sweet was the sound when oft at evening's close*
> *Up yonder hill the village murmur rose."*

Alas, like "The Deserted Village," of which the English poet Goldsmith sang:

> *"But now the sounds of population fail,*
> *No cheerful murmurs fluctuate in the gale,*
> *No busy steps the grass-grown footway tread,*
> *For all the bloomy flush of life is fled."*

Every vestige of Gibsonville and St. Helena has vanished from the earth. The sister villages are merely part of the picturesque landscape now in the Northern part of Letchworth State Park.

Ironically it was water power that gave the villages being. It is remotely possible that one day the waters of the Genesee, impounded by the big Federal flood control dam in the gorge, may close over them. That is why even the bones of the pioneers have been removed from the old village cemeteries. But only the kingsize daddy of all Valley floods could send the waters pouring over the dam spillway in sufficient volume to cover the flats on which the two "deserted villages" stood.

Gibsonville, in the southwest corner of the Town of Leicester, Livingston County, and St. Helena, in the Town of Castile, Wyoming County, were part of the 17,927 acre Gardeau Reservation granted Mary Jemison at the Treaty of Big Tree in 1797.

After The White Woman in 1823 sold most of her vast tract to three pioneers, Micah Brooks, whose name lives in the hilltop hamlet of Brooksgrove; Jellis Clute and Henry B. Gibson, a leading Canandaiguan, the tract was split three ways and opened for settlement. Gibson moved to the Valley and the settlement that sprang up around the falls of the Silver Lake Outlet, also known as Silver Creek, just before that stream empties into the Genesee, took his name.

As early as 1792, that remarkable frontier character, Ebenezer "Indian" Allen, had sensed the power potential of the waterfall in the Outlet and had built a saw mill there. It was, according to historian Lockwood L. Doty, the second saw mill west of the Genesee and it sawed the first boards in the Valley. Indians had to help Allen raise his mill because the white settlers in the region were too few. Within two years Allen left the region for Canada, where he died in 1813.

H. B. Gibson lost no time in selling his lots and in the 1820s the first settlers, most of them of the Yankee stock, came in. A grist mill was built beside the Outlet. Reid Parker of Perry, whose great-grandfather settled in the area in 1823 and whose family has ever since lived around Gibsonville, has located a pair of giant stones which undoubtedly belonged to the pioneer grist mill.

Around the 1840s that grist mill was converted into a paper mill and Gibsonville became an industrial village. Its economy revolved around the paper mill for half a century. Around the mill rose a dozen houses, a combination store-postoffice, a blacksmith shop and the schoolhouse of District No. 9.

The mill under various owners through the years gave employment to most of the citizens of Gibsonville. Most of them also farmed little plots. In 1868 there were 22 families getting their mail from Gibsonville Postoffice which also served the farm families on the nearby hills.

The mill made fine manila, butcher, tea and rice paper from rags and for a nation-wide trade; in early years its wagons scoured the countryside for rags. After a knitting mill was opened in Perry in 1881, the paper mill got its waste rags, hauled down the Creek Road to Gibsonville. Much of the paper mill's finished product was shipped by Genesee Valley Canal in early times and later by railroad. In either case it had to be hauled to nearby ports or stations.

Gibsonville, under the brow of the hill along which the state parkway today follows the course of the old dirt road, was a self-sufficient community, with its paper mill employing at least a dozen hands. Religious services were held in the schoolhouse. Occasionally a traveling medicine show came to town.

Then on Dec. 13, 1894 flames devoured the four-story wooden paper mill. It was a death blow to the industrial community. Slowly Gibsonville went to sleep. Families, even long settled ones like the Hulls, moved out. Deserted houses fell into disrepair. Grass grew over the two streets, Main and

Mill. But the district school kept going until the 1930s, although at the end there was hardly a corporal's guard of pupils.

In the depression-haunted 1930s, a new chapter was written in the story of the ghost town. It became the site of sprawling barracks of a Civilian Conservation Corps, one of the New Deal's happiest experiments. Most of the remaining houses were torn down or moved away. The CCC took over and for years the youths did yeoman work in the woods and in building roads and bridges. Now all that's left of the CCC camp are the ruins of a stone building the Corps built.

With visions of a power dam in the gorge, the Rochester Gas and Electric Corporation early in the 1900s acquired the paper mill site and other properties. It added to its holdings around 1926 when the dream grew clearer. But the private utility dam never came to pass. When the government began its flood control project, Gibsonville became part of the dam's potential reservoir and now it, like the adjoining acreage, is part of the state park.

When Gibsonville's dead were moved to Hope Cemetery in Perry, it was the last act in the drama of the industrial village on the Silver Lake Outlet. Now Gibsonville is "one with Nineveh and Tyre."

*   *   *

St. Helena, named after the bleak isle of Napoleon's captivity, was settled in 1826. The forests were being cut down and the logs were floated on the river. Ambitious pioneers visualized an important town there on the Genesee flatlands between the steep hills. They hired an English engineer to lay out the village into three zones, residential, commercial

140

and industrial. That was a mighty progressive step in the 1820s.

The place had three streets, Main, Water and Maiden Lane. You can still see traces of those thoroughfares although the grass and weeds are taking over and only waddling woodchucks use them these days.

The first St. Helena bridge across the Genesee, linking Wyoming and Livingston Counties, was built in 1835. It was a covered affair with latticework sides. The last iron bridge, which led to the road up the hill into Livingston County, was dismantled in 1950. It had been closed some years before. Now only the stone abutments are there.

A map of 1853 shows several saw mills, a grist mill, a wood working shop. Traces remain of the old mill dam and raceway. In its heyday St. Helena also had a hotel, two general stores, a cider mill, a smithy, 25 dwellings and a school which enrolled 75 pupils. The village sent 22 volunteers to the Civil War.

Its star waned slowly. The mills and business places closed, one by one. Some houses burned. They never were replaced. Villagers moved away and their homes rotted into ruin.

The river kept cutting closer to the settlement. Several times it washed out the bridge and once some farm buildings. By the turn of the century there were only nine families left in St. Helena.

But the little one-story white schoolhouse with the belfry and the green blinds did not give up the ghost until about 1920. It had been the community gathering place for years. There the Methodists had held their services. It had been the scene of funerals, donations, Christmas exercises, patriotic meetings and political rallies that had brought people from Smoky Hollow, Gibsonville, Portageville and other

141

communities. The school house also held nostalgic memories for many men and women scattered throughout the state who had learned their first lessons there.

The last inhabitants moved out in 1948. St. Helena has not been a deserted village so very long. Last to go were Mrs. Nellie Streeter and her son, George. They had lived there 38 years. Mrs. Streeter told me in 1950 a few months before her death those last years "down in the hollow" were pretty lonesome without any neighbors.

The Rochester Gas and Electric Corporation, with the power dam in the Valley in mind, had bought the site of the village in the 1920s and rented the land to the Streeters. It is good land and was intensely cultivated until the last family moved away.

When I walked down the steep hill to St. Helena in the late Spring of 1950, the shell of the Streeter house, a tasteful residence architecturally, still stood and there were other evidences of recent habitation—some collapsed barns, a rickety hay rack, a pile of straw. The old cemetery on the hill above the deserted village was covered with brambles but the headstones were still discernible. The pioneers were sleeping undisturbed.

Now there is nothing amid the lank weeds—except the rotting boards of an old shed—to tell that once a village throbbed there. Even the cemetery is gone from the hill. In 1952 the state took 92 bodies out of St. Helena burying ground and reinterred them in Castile's Grace Cemetery.

Among the bones were those of a man, possibly an Indian, wrapped in animal skins. His identity remains a mystery. Several other bodies could not be identified. For no burials had been made in St. Helena cemetery for more than 80 years. But on some headstones are the names of pioneers—

142

Yankee names like Stocking, Morse, Westbrook, Preston, Smith, Gifford.

Across the roads that once led to the ghost towns of St. Helena and Gibsonville are signs bearing that grim word, "ABANDONED." The two villages where once "health and plenty cheer'd the laboring swain" are abandoned, too. The death of a community is a pathetic thing.

Chapter 12

The Wadsworths

The Wadsworths are the Genesee Valley's most famous family. They have been there 165 years. They were almost the first settlers. Few families have owned so much land in one locality so long.

Few families have made a deeper imprint on a region. Because of the Wadsworths and the other landed gentry that followed them into the Valley, there is, at least in the Geneseo sector, a way of life that is different than that of their Upstate neighbors.

It is the land of the fox hunt, the manor house, the thoroughbred stock, the tenant farm, the family tradition and a political, as well as a land-holding, family dynasty.

But this is not the comic opera English countryside so many have pictured it, the private duchy of the land owners who spend their days riding to hounds and entertaining in the mansions, with the yeomen and the vassals forever pulling their forelocks to the squires.

True there is a fox hunt in the Valley, one of the oldest in the nation. A Wadsworth founded it and through the years most of the clan have followed the pack.

However the Wadsworths cannot be dismissed as hunting squires. Most of them have been serious-minded people with

145

vast business interests and attendant responsibilities. They have successfully operated the oldest system of tenant farming in America. They have brought advanced methods of farming to the Valley and improved the breed of livestock. They had not been absentee landlords. They have lived on the land and given it their personal attention.

Today the two branches of the family own a total of more than 25,000 acres. And the sixth generation is living on Wadsworth land.

Wadsworths have fought in every American war. Two of them were generals and one of those generals died in battle. Another Wadsworth, a private, served with Teddy Roosevelt's Rough Riders.

Generations of the family have been in the public service as legislators and diplomats. It seems strange today that the name of Wadsworth is missing from the roll calls at Albany and at Washington. Two James Wadsworths served a total of more than 50 years in the Congress of the United States.

They went to Ivy League colleges, generally to Yale. They traveled widely and in the best circles. They allied themselves by marriage to other important families. Yet they never lost the common touch. Otherwise would the voters have returned Wadsworths to office year after year?

Geneseo people are proud and actually fond of their first family. They call them by their first names. The Wadsworths mingle in all village affairs. They respond to fire alarms with the other volunteers.

An older generation of villagers was more in awe of the Wadsworths. As a longtime resident put it:

"In the old days the entrance of a Wadsworth lady into a group was likely to bring an awkward silence. Now it brings

146

a chorus of 'Hi, Martha' or whatever the lady's given name may be."

The Wadsworths meet everyone with the friendly courtesy that is the acme of good manners. They are not pretentious people. They are informal in attire but they wear even their farm clothes with an air. After all they were *born* to the manor. Overdressed "Johnnies Come Lately" can never master that easy grace.

It is of some significance that the motto on the family coat of arms is a Latin phrase which means: "The eagle does not catch flies." The Wadsworths of the Valley have always operated on the grand scale.

Probably I shall be accused of pulling my own forelock (had I one) to the squires. I am only trying to set the picture straight—to present the Wadsworths as substantial, essentially democratic people, with more wealth, land and traditions than most folks, but still not merely puppets in an unreal and stilted "Merrie England" pageant set in an Upstate rural countryside.

*   *   *

The Wadsworths are of English stock. The name originally meant Woods Court.

Among the 123 passengers on the ship *Lion* from England which docked at Boston on Sept. 16, 1632 was a William Wadsworth, head of a family of four. He was the first of the line in America and four years after his arrival he was one of the founders of Hartford, Conn.

His son Joseph attained fame on the night of Oct. 31, 1687. A new Royal governor, Sir Edmund Andros, had come to wrest its cherished charter from the crown colony of Connecticut. A session of the Assembly was called and the charter laid on the table. Just then every candle in the room went out. When they were relighted the charter had disappeared. Joseph Wadsworth had seized it and hidden it in a great tree, known thereafter as the Charter Oak. Sir Edmund was thwarted and the charter was saved.

Another Connecticut Wadsworth, Jeremiah, became an important man in the Revolution, as a commissary general. He was a wealthy Federalist and a friend of Washington and Hamilton. When the Bay State speculators, Phelps and Gorham, made their vast purchase of wild York State lands, he bought 4,000 acres in the Genesee Country.

Jeremiah Wadsworth, too old to settle on his purchase, offered two young nephews, James and William, of Durham, Conn., one-half interest in the lands and told James he could have the agency of the other half if he would go to the Genesee.

Both brothers decided to go and contracted for 2,000 acres of wild land along the Genesee they had never seen for eight cents an acre or $160.

James, then 22, was a graduate of Yale and had taught school in Montreal. William was seven years his senior but had not seen as much of the world. They had inherited some $10,000 apiece from their father.

In the Spring of 1790 the two young Connecticut Yankees began the long journey to the Genesee. William, with two hired men, the family Negress Jenny, an ox cart and three yoke of oxen, started across country for Albany. James, the business man, went to New York to buy supplies. He went by sloop from New York to Albany. Aboard he met a fur trader with a Teutonic accent named John Jacob Astor. The chance acquaintance ripened into a friendship that lasted the rest of their lives.

148

The brothers met at Albany. James made the rest of the trip by the waterways and William with his ox cart through the woods. West of Whitesville he had to make his own road most of the way to Canandaigua, the capital of the Phelps and Gorham Purchase. There he again met James and the pair started for their new home. After camping overnight near the foot of Conesus Lake, they parted again, James going on horseback down the Indian trail to the Genesee, William by slower ox cart. William got lost in a swamp and spent the night there. Meanwhile James had found the chosen home site, about where the village high school now stands, just west of the present Geneseo. It was the 10th of June, 1790.

Work was begun at once on a log house and until it was finished all slept in the cart or on the ground. The ring of axes brought to the scene Lemuel Jennings, the first white settler in Geneseo. For two years this big frontiersman had been herding cattle for Oliver Phelps on the lush Genesee Flats.

James had business in Canandaigua the second day in the Valley and on the way home got lost until he saw a light in a clearing. It was the candle Jenny was holding for brother William as he hewed planks for the new house.

In September of 1790 the Genesee Fever, that malarial ailment which so plagued the early settlers, laid low all the Wadsworth household except Jenny.

The Wadsworths bought 4,000 more acres of Valley land, paying the company price, 50 cents an acre. A few settlers drifted into the region and the Wadsworth settlement became known as Big Tree, the name of an Indian chief and an Indian village.

The Wadsworths of Big Tree became widely known on

149

Picture by Katherine Merrill

Under the Oaks on a Wadsworth Estate

as well as a land holder. The commission he received from sales of the Pulteney tract and other lands enabled him and his brother to increase their Valley holdings until they were operating one of the largest estates in America.

James evolved the farm tenancy system which still endures. "Anti-rent wars" ended the reign of the patroons in the Hudson Valley but because the Wadsworth plan was more flexible and the proprietors more lenient, there was no trouble in the Genesee Valley.

Lack of cash gave rise to the tenancy system whereby the rental was paid in wheat—delivered to a Wadsworth mill. The tenant had to pay all the taxes, could not assign his lease, had to keep up buildings and fences, plant certain designated crops and apple trees and to turn back into the soil forage crops in the form of manure. Some of the clauses still remain in the leases.

At first these leases were for life. In 1809 an annual renewal plan was adopted. The tenant received a house, barns and 40 cows. He was to take care of the buildings, cut the hay and retain half of the butter and cheese, the other half going to the landlord who also retained all the calves.

The Wadsworth plan insured stable tenants, not fly-by-nighters and two, sometimes three, generations of tenants have lived on the same farms. The Wadsworths helped their tenants in times of adversity, such as the drought year of 1806 when James wrote to Robert Troup, the Pulteney land agent:

"I am supporting three or four families and expect to be called on by more soon. My brother has been compelled to turn 50 fat oxen from our stables to preserve for poor families the grain they were consuming."

In 1804 James married Naomi Wolcott of an upper crust

151

Connecticut family. His aristocratic bride did not have to live in the log cabin which had failed to please the Duke de Liancourt nor in the little cobblestone house which succeeded it. Around 1800 the Home Place had been built, on the southern edge of Geneseo village. Two stories and an attic were added later. It is the present Homestead, for many years the residence of the William Wadsworth branch of the family.

Into it went the massive oaken timbers that today are the despair of electricians and plumbers, as the present master of the Homestead, William P. Wadsworth, will tell you.

The Wadsworths were progressive, pioneering farmers. They raised hemp and flax on the moist river flats. They tried raising tobacco. They grew corn until wheat became the great Valley crop. They even had their own brand of flour and "Wadsworth Flour," ground in Wadsworth mills, brought a premium in the market.

They imported young mules from New England and after the animals had matured, sold them to Southern tobacco growers. They bought Kentucky and Indiana cattle and fattened them for sale. They imported Merino sheep and at one time were called the greatest sheep and wool producers in the nation. Their acreage multiplied as James pooled his land agent fees with the proceeds of the farms his brother managed.

The brothers were active in civic affairs. William served several terms as town supervisor. In the War of 1812 he volunteered his services as a major general of militia. When General Van Rensselaer was wounded at Queenstown, Wadsworth succeeded to the American command. The engagement was lost only because of the lack of reinforcements. He was taken prisoner and came home on parole. There never was any question of the bronzed Bill's personal bravery or his ability to handle men.

James Wadsworth early sensed the possibilities of Rochester and once expressed the wish that "the tract of 100 acres (a large part of the present downtown Rochester) could be bought from the Maryland gentlemen. The bridge and mill seat render it very valuable indeed." He founded a settlement at the Rapids, opposite the present University of Rochester River Campus which was called Castle Town. The Erie Canal doomed it as a potential port.

The Wadsworths owned so much land at one time that there was a saying that they could ride all the way from Geneseo to Rochester on a highway bordered by their own land. It was almost true.

The brothers, James and William, gave the site of the jail and court house when Livingston County was formed in 1821 and were instrumental in making Geneseo the shire town over the claims of Avon and Lakeville.

James Wadsworth shrank from active politics although he exerted much influence. He was proposed as the Anti-Masonic candidate for United States Senator and for governor in 1828 but he did not encourage the boom and his name was withdrawn.

His prime interest was in education and he may well be called one of the fathers of the common school system. He was a pioneer advocate of district school libraries. He supplied books and lecturers for such libraries out of his own purse. He had tracts distributed at his own expense on educational matters. He urged the establishment of teacher training schools.

He pushed enactment of the school library law in 1838, founded the Geneseo Athenaeum which became the present

153

Wadsworth Library and induced his friend Astor to build the magnificent Public Library in New York City. He gave the land on which the cobblestone schoolhouse of District 5 was built on Geneseo's Center Street in 1835. That building now houses the County Historical Center-Museum. In its rear is part of the trunk of the Big Tree, the giant oak that stood on the original Wadsworth land and under which the treaty of 1797 was signed. During his lifetime James Wadsworth contributed nearly $100,000 to the cause of education.

Maj. Gen. William Wadsworth died in 1833, leaving his share in the vast family estate to his brother's children.

James Wadsworth, the pioneer who had come to the Valley in 1790 and lived in a log cabin, died in his Geneseo mansion in 1844, one of America's greatest land owners. He left four children: Harriet, who married Martin Brimmer, onetime mayor of Boston; Elizabeth, the wife of Charles Augustus Murray, son of an English earl; James Samuel and William Wolcott.

The bulk of the estate went to the two sons. That is another family tradition. Each son founded a distinctive branch of the clan. Four generations of James Wadsworths, each devoted to public service, have lived in the manor house at the northern end of Geneseo. The fourth William Wadsworth is now master of the Homestead, at the southern end of the village. His grandchildren represent the sixth generation at the "Home Place."

*　　*　　*

In the Valley James S. Wadsworth is always referred to as "the General." He was born in 1809, studied at Yale and Harvard and read law in the Boston office of Daniel Webster. But he never practiced. He was occupied with managing his large estate. In the 1840s he made new investments in Michigan and Indiana lands. Those lands were sold off to settlers at a considerable profit before the Civil War.

It was James S. Wadsworth who in 1835 built stately Hartford House for his bride, Mary Craig Wharton of Philadelphia. In its design the young couple copied Lord Hartford's villa in Regent Park during a honeymoon visit to England. The house has a three-story central unit and two wings and overlooks a broad sweep of the Valley.

About the same time he built the nearby office on Geneseo's Main Street diagonally opposite the Courthouse. There the affairs of the estate are handled today by the General's great-grandson, Reverdy, in the office in which have sat three generations of his forebears.

James S. Wadsworth had many interests. He was the first president of the State Agricultural Society and a regent of the State University. He brought a Kentucky bull to the Valley to improve the breed. When the weevil ruined the wheat crop, he let many of his tenants fall heavily in arrears. In 1844 he sent a ship load of corn to famine-stricken Ireland.

He was a firm opponent of slavery and left the Democratic Party to support Martin Van Buren and the Free Soil ticket in 1848 and he never returned to the fold. He was an early leader in the new Republican Party and became a member of the so-called Radical wing which would not compromise on the slavery question.

Wadsworth was a member of the futile Peace Congress of 1861. Later that year he spurred the raising of a regiment in Livingston County which was named in his honor "the

Wadsworth Guards." Officially it was the 104th Regiment of New York Volunteers.

He himself enlisted as a volunteer. Governor Morgan had named him major general of state volunteers but the federal officials did not recognize state commissions.

So the Genesee grandee at the age of 53 appeared on the staff of General McDowell as a volunteer aide, a sort of glorified message bearer, with the rank of major. He distinguished himself under fire at the first Battle of Bull Run. Soon he was commissioned a major general and assigned to a command in the Army of the Potomac.

At the very outset of the war, he had distinguished himself in another way. On April 9, 1861, when Washington was surrounded by enemies, almost isolated by the destruction of bridges between Philadelphia and Baltimore and hostile mobs lined the streets of the Maryland metropolis, Wadsworth chartered a ship in New York, loaded it with supplies at his own expense and personally conducted it to troops stranded at Annapolis.

In March, 1862, General Wadsworth was given the difficult post of military governor of Washington. He and other Radical leaders, fearing the capital might be invaded by the raiding Stonewall Jackson, induced President Lincoln to withdraw two divisions from McClellan's Peninsular campaign to defend Washington, an action which contributed to "Little Mac's" failure to take Richmond.

That same year the New York Republicans, over the opposition of the old boss, Thurlow Weed and with the support of Horace Greeley, nominated Wadsworth as its candidate for governor. He ran on a "win-the-war" program. His opponent, Horatio Seymour, an anti-war Democrat, won by 10,000 votes. Weed was ever cool to the Geneseo general and prevented his later nomination for the United States Senate.

General Wadsworth was called back into the field in December of 1862 as a division commander and fought at Chancellorsville and Gettysburg. After Gettysburg and Grant's capture of Vicksburg he made an inspection tour of the Mississippi Valley, reporting on the freedmen's camps and the condition of liberated slaves there.

Early in 1864 he served in Washington as a commissioner for the exchange of prisoners. Then he went back into the field, again as commander of a division. He was fatally wounded while leading a charge on the third day of the bloody battle of the Wilderness. Two days later, on May 8, 1864, he died in a Confederate hospital. A Virginian, living in the neighborhood, provided a coffin and buried the general in his own private plot until the remains could be taken back to the Valley.

Geneseo was draped in mourning for the military funeral. In the family plot in Temple Hill Cemetery, his is the only ornate tombstone. It is a granite block, 8 feet long and 10 feet high, ornamented with flag-draped urn, cannon, sword, epaulets and laurel wreath, along with the names of the battles in which General Wadsworth fought. Most of the others sleep under simple, old fashioned raised tablets.

The General's three sons, Charles F., Craig W., and James Wolcott, all served in the Civil War.

The General's brother, William W., of the Home Farm, died in 1852 at the age of 42. He married a Boston Austin and was the pioneering type. He tried to invent a mowing machine and he founded a short-lived agricultural or manual labor school in Geneseo, under which poor pupils were virtually indentured for an eight-year period of farming study.

W. W. raised beef cattle, fattening the young stock his

buyers got from the Southern Tier for two years on the river flats before marketing them along the Eastern Seaboard.

His three sons, William Austin, Livingston, who died at the age of 16, and Herbert, were all too young for service in the Civil War.

For a brief period Craig Wadsworth was associated with his brother, William W., in the management of the Homestead estate. He died in Philadelphia at an early age, leaving two sons. One of them, Craig W., still lives in Geneseo. At 81 he is the patriarch of the clan and a highly respected resident of the Valley. He served in the Spanish-American War with the Rough Riders, whose colonel, Theodore Roosevelt, on being elected governor, made Wadsworth a member of his military staff.

In the early 1900s he began a long and distinguished diplomatic career with the American legation in England. Later he held posts in Lima, Peru, and in Persia.

His brother, James Samuel (Jim Sam) died in 1930 but he is well remembered in the Valley as a popular, jovial and uninhibited hunting squire, a World War I commander, a familiar figure at horse shows who was at one time joint master of the Genesee Valley Fox Hounds. The colorful Jim Sam never took farming too seriously.

Getting back to the General's sons in the rather complicated skein of Wadsworth genealogy, Charles F. settled in the Town of York on what is now the Westerly estate of his grandson, Porter Chandler, a New York lawyer who spends his Summers in the Valley.

*   *   *

The General's other son, James Wolcott Wadsworth, Sr., became the master of Hartford House, manager of vast estates and a national figure in politics. He left Yale in 1864 after his father's death and although only 17, became an aide on the staff of General Warren in the Army of the Potomac.

After the war, the young veteran played first base and pitched for the Geneseo baseball nine, the Livingstons. All his life he was interested in baseball and in the 1890s was the "angel" for the Geneseo team which once boasted several college stars in its lineup, among them his son, "Young Jim" Wadsworth, who played first base.

In 1876 James W., Sr., married Louise Travers of New York, a cousin of the Jenny Jerome who became Lady Churchill and the mother of Britain's former prime minister, Sir Winston.

Wadsworth entered politics early in life and at the foot of the ladder—as town supervisor. Then he went to the State Assembly and in 1879 he was elected state comptroller, the youngest man to hold the office up to that time. He was 33.

He was first elected to Congress in 1881 and for more than 20 years represented a rock-ribbed Republican district in the Lower House. Older Valley people still speak of him as "the Congressman."

While keeping a close eye on his farms and his cattle, of which he was an excellent judge, he built up a sturdy political machine, which he passed on to his son, "Young Jim." He marshalled the considerable Italian-American vote in his district to augment the hereditary Republican legions.

The Congressman with his iron gray mane and generous mustache and his courtly bearing, was a just and kind-hearted man but he was sometimes a bit imperious, too. There was no question that he was the boss, not only of his estate but of his political bailiwick.

159

In Congress he was allied with the Republican Old Guard and was one of Speaker Joe Cannon's most able and reliable lieutenants. The Wadsworths never had much use for reformers and Congressman Wadsworth in 1906 crossed swords with that master opportunist, Theodore Roosevelt, then in the White House.

Wadsworth was chairman of the powerful Agricultural Committee of the House which investigated packing house conditions following Upton Sinclair's expose in his book, *The Jungle*. Sinclair sought to awaken the American people to the deplorable living conditions of the packing house workers but succeeded only in stirring them up over his revelations of filth in the stockyards and the adulteration of the meat they ate.

TR and other reformers thought that Wadsworth, in conducting the hearings, minimized the threat of packing house methods to the health of the workers and of the consumers. When he brought out a substitute bill in place of the one TR wanted, an exchange of bitter letters ensued between the President and the Congressman.

The principal bone of contention was that Wadsworth's bill made the government, not the packers, pay the costs of inspection. The Wadsworth Pure Food Bill passed and went into effect July 1, 1906.

Roosevelt was then at the height of his popularity and the row with the President did not help the Geneseo Congressman in the Fall election. In a stunning upset the veteran Wadsworth was defeated by Peter A. Porter, an independent, running on the Democratic ticket. Porter made the most of the meat issue. He used a cow as his campaign emblem and plastered his district, which included populous Niagara County, with posters of "Bossy."

160

Wadsworth went into retirement with no kindly feelings toward TR. When in 1907 the President removed as collector of the Port of Rochester a Wadsworth henchman, Archie D. Sanders of Stafford, the former Congressman castigated the President in these words:

"The whole thing stamps the President as unreliable, a faker and a humbug. For years he has indulged in lofty sentiments and violates them all for the sake of satisfying his petty spite. Thank God, he can't fool all the people all of the time and the country is fast awakening to the real character of the bloody hero of Kettle Hill."

*   *   *

The old Congressman lived to see his only son, James Wolcott Wadsworth, Jr. scale the national political heights.

"Young Jim" was born in 1877. He went to private school and, of course, to Yale. At Yale he played a star first base and in the Summers of the middle 1890s he played all over Western New York with the Geneseo team of college all-stars his father sponsored.

Early in life he was taught the rudiments of farming. His father sent him to "the Street farm" to learn from the Wadsworth tenant there. The family's chief stableman taught the boy how to groom a horse. One Summer he worked in the village bank. That, too, was part of his apprenticeship in management of the great estate that would one day be his.

Young Wadsworth volunteered as a private in the Spanish-American War. His light artillery outfit got only as far as Porto Rico. After his discharge—as a private—"Young Jim" sailed on a transport with units of the Regular Army for the Philippines as a civilian. In the islands as an aide to an infantry colonel, he was under fire. His military experience, brief as it was, proved helpful in later years to the chairman of the Senate's Military Affairs Committee.

Wadsworth made his first political speech in 1900. He talked on good roads at a picnic held at Brooksgrove. In the national campaign of that year he organized a mounted marching club, which rode some 300 miles that Autumn. It won the praise of Rough Rider Teddy Roosevelt, candidate for Vice President, who addressed a Geneseo rally in the campaign.

In the Summer of 1902 "Young Jim" risked his life to save a herd of 160 prize steers trapped in a river flood. That Autumn he married Alice, daughter of John Hay, McKinley's secretary of state who had married into the wealthy Whitney clan. The young couple spent two winters in Washington and mingled in the top echelon of capital society and officialdom.

In 1904, at the behest of his father, young Wadsworth made his first run for public office as a candidate for the Assembly. The voters liked this tall, broad-shouldered balding chap with the cordial folksy ways and the ready grin. He won handsomely.

He was only a second-year man and only 28 years old when he was chosen Speaker of the Assembly in a rousing struggle for power between his backer, Governor Higgins, and former Governor Odell. The young Speaker soon won the respect and liking of members on both sides of the aisle.

Wadsworth took a liking to a ruddy, cigar-smoking and then obscure young Tammany Assemblyman named Alfred E. Smith and assigned the East Sider to some good committees. The friendship between the two men, so unlike in background, continued during their lifetimes.

The Speaker displayed his independent spirit in 1907 when

he braved the combined wrath of former President Roosevelt, the then President Taft and the then Governor Hughes by opposing the state-wide direct primary. He felt that the system would not do away with bosses but merely lessen their responsibility to the public. He lost that fight but in a few years saw the state amend the direct primary law to restore the old convention system of choosing nominees for state office. Ironically Jim Wadsworth in 1914 was the first man to be nominated for United States Senator under the direct primary plan.

In 1911 Wadsworth had retired from the Assembly to manage his aunt's large ranch in Texas and he was there when the call came in 1914 to run for the Senate as a successor to Elihu Root, who was retiring.

Wadsworth won easily over the Democratic candidate, James W. Gerard, United States ambassador to Germany, who also had been born in Geneseo although his parents were New Yorkers. When he entered the Senate, his party was in the minority. Woodrow Wilson was President and the Southern Democrats were running the show. The new Senator was assigned to the Military Affairs Committee. It was an important post because of the overseas war and one to Jim's liking. In 1913 he had been instrumental in organizing a Cavalry troop of the National Guard in Geneseo. He was made its first lieutenant and every week during the Winter of 1915 he traveled back Upstate to attend the drills.

As a Senator he voted with his party on domestic issues. After the declaration of war, he forgot politics, as he did in a later war and in another Congress, and supported the administration's war policies. He helped work out the draft act of 1917 and after the Republicans won control of Congress in 1918, he became chairman of Military Affairs and was the principal author of the National Defense Act of 1920.

Because he believed that the League of Nations Covenant "sacrificed the independence of the United States," he opposed both the Wilson League and treaty. He wrote two reservations to the treaty and voted for all the drastic Lodge reservations in the face of heavy pressure from Republican pro-Leaguers.

Jim Wadsworth was never one to shift to the popular side of an issue just to get votes. A fellow legislator said of him that he never lost his convictions or his temper. As a speaker he was no rabble rouser and used no rhetorical flourishes. He talked with force and clarity, almost in a conversational tone, to the point and without any groping for words. That engaging smile which creased his face into a thousand wrinkles charmed his audiences.

His stand against woman suffrage cost him votes. But he was convinced that the method of adopting constitutonal amendments by vote of state legislatures, rather than by popular referendum, was wrong. It also happened that his wife was a leader of the anti-suffrage forces.

He was unfaltering in his opposition to prohibition, which he believed was sumptuary legislation, impossible of enforcement. His convictions cost him his seat in the Senate but events vindicated his stand.

The election of 1920 which swept his handsome and weak fellow Senator, Warren G. Harding, into the Presidency, brought Wadsworth an easy re-election victory. One wonders if the Geneseo man did not come to rue the part he played in putting Harding over on the Republican convention of '20.

The early 1920s were the glory years for Wadsworth. He was the "Mr. Republican" of the Empire State and at the

1924 state convention in Rochester he virtually dictated the ticket headed by Theodore Roosevelt, Jr., a losing ticket, by the way.

When the campaign of 1926 rolled around, Senator Wadsworth had to face two opponents, the popular New York City Democrat, Bob Wagner, and a "dry" nonenity. The "drys" drew off enough votes to defeat Wadsworth and retire him to private life. The wiseacres said "Jim is all done."

In 1932 the Republicans of the 39th District met in Rochester to name their candidate for Congress. It was expected that the veteran Archie Sanders would again be the nominee. A smiling former United States Senator electrified the reporters by announcing that the candidate would be James Wadsworth of Geneseo. Sanders, an old Wadsworth hand, had heard "his master's voice."

So Jim Wadsworth went back to Washington and the public service. Only two other men in history have served in the Lower House after being Senators. John Quincy Adams and Theodore E. Burton of Ohio.

As in 1914, Wadsworth found himself in the minority party. He was no longer "Young Jim" but an elder statesman. Up in the Valley they still called him "Senator."

Wadsworth disliked the New Deal. He was opposed to any regimentation and the spending of public funds "to get votes." I can still hear the honest indignation in his voice when speaking at a 19th Ward rally in Rochester he said: "I resent these bureaucrats who are telling me how much and what I can plant—on my own land!"

But when war clouds lowered, Wadsworth, as he had in an earlier world conflict, forsook partisanship to work for a strong America. He was co-sponsor of the Burke-Wadsworth Selective Service Act and he never wavered in his support

165

of the prosecution of the war. When only four months before Pearl Harbor, the fate of the extension of the draft hung in the balance. Wadsworth rallied enough Republican votes to save it. Arthur Krock of the New York *Times* wrote that "Mr. Wadsworth has come to be recognized as the conscience of the House."

In the Summer of 1950 Wadsworth announced that he would not be a candidate for Congress again. He gave no reasons. Only his family knew of his grave illness.

James W. Wadsworth died in Washington in 1952. No native of the Valley had ever risen to higher place. None possessed in fuller measure the liking and respect of his neighbors. There was something Churchillian about this landed gentleman whose character was as sturdy as the oaks that dot his lands.

High officialdom attended the funeral in Washington. Among the mourners at the rites in Geneseo were many humble people, too. Some of them like their fathers before them had been tenants on Wadsworth lands—and they had liked "Young Jim."

*   *   *

His elder son, James Jeremiah (Jerry to the Valley) went to Yale. He played baseball at Yale and with the Geneseo team, first base, of course.

Like his grandsire and his father, he served in the State Assembly—from 1931 to 1941. During World War II he was an industral relations executive for a Buffalo airplane company. Since 1946 he has held a variety of government jobs. At one time he was acting national director of civil defense. Since 1950 he has held a lofty post, that of deputy United States representative to the United Nations. He resides in

Photo by Pearl Stutz, Democrat and Chronicle

Genesee Valley Fox Hunt

Courtesy The Catholic Courier-Journal

"Cowled Farmers" at Eventide Beside the Genesee

Washington but comes back to the Valley to vote and sometimes for the Fall hunting.

Evelyn, the former Senator's only daughter, is the wife of W. Stuart Symington, Democratic senator from Missouri. In the early 1930s she displayed the traditional Wadsworth independence of spirit by singing in a New York night club under the name of Eve Symington. New York cafe society liked her and her voice.

The younger son, Reverdy, named after Reverdy Johnson, an ancestor who was attorney general under President Taylor, manages his late father's estates and lives in Geneseo, but not in Hartford House. He resides in a charming white house with green blinds on Center Street, across from Craig Wadsworth's similar colonial type home.

His widowed mother, the daughter of John Hay, lives in Hartford House when she is in the Valley. She spends most of her Winters in Washington. It is a Wadsworth tradition that the parents occupy the manor house as long as one of them lives. Only on the death of both does the son move in.

Reverdy Wadsworth, like his sister, married into a prominent Democratic family, the Roosevelts no less. His wife was Eleanor, daughter of Henry Latrobe Roosevelt, who was assistant secretary of the navy under his kinsman, FDR.

Geneseo people call Reverdy "Rev" just as they greet his cousin, William Perkins Wadsworth, head of the other family branch at the other end of the village, as "Bill." Both belong to the local volunteer fire department and both have served in the local National Guard unit. Both went overseas during World War II.

Reverdy bears a striking resemblance to his father in the Senator's "Young Jim" days. He has his father's easy cordiality of manner.

The family estate which he manages comprises 24 farms in two counties, Livingston and Monroe, and more than 12,000 acres. Two thirds of that acreage is in tenant farms. In 1932 the Senator acquired 7,500 acres from Mrs. Herbert Wadsworth after her husband's death. At that time Howard Gott, who was the Herbert Wadsworth farm agent, joined the Senator's staff. He is still the agent for the estate.

The office in the small lemon-colored building at Main and North Streets is an interesting place and full of mementoes of the past. The years have not changed it much. Frank Luttenton is the office manager as he was in the Senator's time. William L. Olmstead has his insurance office in the building. His father, William L. S., was a Wadsworth farm agent.

In a closet, along with old fashioned pigeon-hole files, like a little village postoffice, stands the strong box that General Wadsworth took with him to the Civil War. In Reverdy's office the stuffed head of a buffalo that Congressman Wadsworth shot while hunting with Buffalo Bill Cody on the plains in the 1870's, looks down upon the scene.

There are pictures on the walls of the Geneseo town team which the old Congressman sponsored and on which "Young Jim" played; an autographed portrait of President Taft, a copy of the declaration of war on Germany in 1917, a letter of appreciation of the Senator's services from Dwight Davis, secretary of war, and other keepsakes which had belonged to James W. Wadsworth, Jr., and his public life.

On the wall of the front office is a framed notice dated March, 1809, captioned "A Notice to New Settlers." In it the first James Wadsworth offered to settlers 60,000 acres of land mostly in Western Monroe County, "near the landing in Fall Town (the present Rochester) on the west side of the Genesee."

The land is described as "remarkably healthy" with no mountains or ledges, abounding in elm, butternut, black ash and walnut trees and adapted to the "raising of hemp and the growing of peaches, apricots and nectarines."

James Wadsworth was fishing for New England settlers in 1809 for he offered "to exchange a few of his lots" on the frontier for "improved farms" in the stony New England hllls.

I saw, too, in that old office, a map book, big as an oldtime atlas of the world, which showed in detail every plot on every Wadsworth farm. It was of the vintage of the early 1890s. Older tenant farmers recall when the agent would come to their homes, lay out the big map book on a table and discuss with the tenant just what crops would be planted in each plot the next season.

*　*　*

The national spotlight never swung so brightly on the William Wadsworth branch of the family. The Homestead people never went in for politics. They stuck to managing their estates, to breeding fine horses, cattle and dogs—and to the Fox Hunt which one of them fathered and supported during his lifetime.

It was William Austin Wadsworth "the Major" in Valley nomenclature, who in 1876 with Charles Carroll Fitzhugh and Judge Lockwood Doty, founded the Genesee Valley Hunt and who supported it for many years. He was Master of Fox Hounds until his death in 1918.

The white and rambling manor house, the Homestead, through the years has opened its doors to followers of the ancient sport of fox hunting. Some of them have been famous people. Because Austin Wadsworth was so closely connected with the Genesee Valley Hunt, he will figure importantly in a later chapter.

He was a public spirited citizen. He gave the memorial drinking fountain with the figure of a bear that is a landmark of downtown Geneseo. He imported pheasants and a game keeper to the Valley in 1890. He sought constantly to improve the breed of Valley livestock. He was a determined man. In the 1870s he wanted the Homestead moved back from the road to its present location. It was a big moving job, too much for two contractors who "went broke" on it. Nothing daunted, the Major had the big mansion put on rollers and gathered 50 yoke of oxen to move it.

At the age of 51 he became a major of volunteers in the War with Spain and saw service in the Philippines. He kept bachelor's hall at the Homestead until his marriage late in life to handsome Elizabeth Perkins, of Boston, 22 years his junior.

She survived the Major by nearly a quarter of a century. She shared her husband's tastes and had much to do with reviving the Genesee Valley Hunt and keeping it going after his death. She also capably administered the big estate until their son, William Perkins, became of age and took over.

William P. Wadsworth, "Bill" to the whole Valley where he is popular alike among grooms and squires, now is master, not only of the Homestead and its 13,500 acres but he also is Master of Fox Hounds, as was his father before him. With the exception of five years (1941–1945) when he was in the military service, he has been the MFH since 1933. After long service in the local Cavalry troop which went overseas as the

101st Mechanized cavalry in World War II, he holds the rank of lieutenant colonel in the inactive reserve.

He is a slender, graying man with bright blue eyes and a quiet, pleasant manner. He also is a mighty busy man. He manages more than 30 farms, three of which he operates himself. The others are farmed by tenants. Also he is the spark plug of the Genesee Valley Hunt. When he is not dashing around to his farms, he is breaking trails in the woods for the coming Hunt, exercising its pack of hounds or working in his office.

He has no agent. He recalled that once his father had four. His office secretary is Miss Betty Andrews, whose late father, Harry Andrews, was for many years the hunstman for the Genesee Valley Hunt, and who herself was once one of "the whips."

Bill Wadsworth's office is older than the one at the other end of town. It was built early in the 19th Century by the two pioneering Wadsworth brothers and it houses files that go back to that time. They are in neat rows on the shelves, each labeled "letters" and "vouchers," one for each of nearly 150 years.

The office is under old trees on the Homestead grounds, between the two drives, the one that sweeps past the gate-keeper's house, marked "for guests" and the other "service drive." Like the James Wadsworth office, it is devoid of frills and it whispers of bygone years. In those two offices of the landed gentry time almost seems to stand still—they are little corners of the Valley the years have changed but little.

In the William Wadsworth office in a cabinet and under glass are two exceedingly rare documents. They are letters and the signatures on them are "Daniel Boone" and "D. Crockett." The latter would bring a fancy price in this

Crockett year of 1955. Neither is for sale. They have been in the possession of the Wadsworth family for more than a century. Bill Wadsworth does not know how they came into the hands of his ancestors.

The Boone letter, dated May 27, 1795, and addressed to a Mr. Williams or Williamson, is hard to decipher. It has to do with the names of certain Kentucky "cricks." Old Daniel wrote in part:

"Agreeable to your request, I send these lines. The south fork of the Kentucky first went by the name of Goos Crick. For proof I have several entrys in May, 1780, by the name of Goos Crick. . . . The names of the small cricks coming in to Goos Crick on the south . . . were given in 1769 by me and by company."

Davy Crockett wrote his letter from Washington City on Jan. 28, 1834 when he was a member of Congress. It is legible and its phrasing would seem to disprove any allegations that the frontiersman was hardly literate. It also indicates considerable business acumen.

Crockett, in reply to an offer made by a publishing firm, Carey & Hart, for the copyrights to his autobiography, first apologized for not answering sooner "because I have been unwell, a considerable part of the time confined to my bed."

Then getting to the point, Davy wrote: "On the subject of your proposal to purchase the copyrights of my book, I cannot think of acceding to it. I believe I can safely say that in one hour I could get five times the amount of your offer without leaving the city."

After some speculation on the possible profits from the book, the author asked: "What part of the clear profit would you allow me?"

Turning down a visit to New York for a conference with

172

the publishers, the Tennessee Congressman explained: "The Deposits question is still under discussion and I am afraid to be absent for fear the vote might be taken on it and when it is taken, I want to be found standing up to the rack but I am a little afraid I won't find much fodder in it."

I am, gentlemen, most respectfully
Your Ob't, very humble servant,
D. Crockett.

The subjects discussed in the Boone and Crockett epistles are not especially weighty but the signatures are valuable indeed.

The three farms of the estate which W. P. operates himself account for 2,500 of the total 13,500 acres. Bill and his wife, the former Martha Scofield, have a son, William Austin, now in college, who is being trained to manage the estate as his father was.

Both Reverdy and William P. Wadsworth firmly believe in the tenant farm system their forebears instituted in the Valley 150 years ago. The annual lease prevents them from getting stuck with a worthless tenant for more than a year. The system whereby the tenant pays the taxes, which is merely a form of rent, gives him a feeling of responsibility and a deeper interest in the farm he works.

Wadsworth tenants have become town officials and generally are substantial people in their community. The third generation of tenants is on one Wadsworth farm. There are several on which the second generation is living. There has never been any serious landlord-tenant trouble in the Valley. The system has endured there longer than in any other part of America.

*   *   *

Once there was another important Wadsworth estate—Ashantee of the Herbert Wadsworths, just south of Avon on the Geneseo Road.

Herbert, son of William W. and brother of William Austin Wadsworth, in 1881 built a fine manor house of stone near the Triphammer Falls of the Conesus Outlet. It was set, like all Wadsworth mansions, behind a thick screen of shrubbery. It was named Ashantee. Some say that was just a fancy pioneer name for "shanty."

Herbert Wadsworth, like brother Austin, married a woman some years his junior. She was Martha Blow of Missouri and she was one of the most accomplished horsewomen in America. In 1910 she rode 212 miles in 19 hours and 20 minutes in an endurance test. In 1912 she rode 900 miles on horseback from Washington to Ashantee via West Virginia. It set some kind of a record.

The Herbert Wadsworths did much to improve the breed of Valley hunters. In 1913 they brought in Wonder Boy, 4-year-old red thoroughbred, the largest stallion in America. Mrs. Wadsworth founded the Valley Breeders Association and promoted shows at Avon Springs. She built at Ashantee a huge riding hall of steel and concrete with tanbark floor. Her husband used to drive an elegant four-in-hand to the Hunt doings in Geneseo. In his late years he lived much at his North Carolina estate.

Shortly after Herbert Wadsworth's death in 1927, his widow sold the 7,000-acre estate to Senator Wadsworth, reserving the mansion and 20 acres around it. It was called the biggest real estate deal in the Valley since Indian times.

Martha Blow Wadsworth, equestrienne extraordinary, died in 1934. The present owner is her niece, Elena, wife of Michael Moukanhoff, erstwhile lieutenant of the Imperial

Russian army and a fervent anti-vivisectionist. Now the place is up for sale, mansion, riding hall, saw mill, creamery, waterfalls and all.

*   *   *

At the main entrance of Geneseo's Temple Hill cemetery sleep generations of Wadsworths—the pioneering brothers, the polished James and the bluff Bill; the General, the Congressman, the Senator, the Major, Herbert of Ashantee, Charles of Westerly, Jim Sam who got so much fun out of life, and the rest.

The Wadsworth burial plot behind its stout iron fence and under spreading elms is impressive, although most of the stones are modest enough.

In life, those sleeping Wadsworths cast massive shadows over their Valley, where now the sixth generation of the clan is carrying on the Wadsworth traditions.

Chapter 13

Boots and Saddles

"The dusky night rides down the sky,
And ushers in the morn;
The hounds all join in glorious cry,
The huntsman winds his horn,
And a-hunting we will go."

An Englishman, Henry Fielding, wrote those lines in the 18th Century about the time fox hunting was getting to be the rage among the county families in the English Midlands.

For almost 80 Autumns now the Genesee Valley has echoed to that same glorious cry of the hounds and blast of the huntsman's horn. The Genesee Valley Fox Hunt is the fourth oldest in America.

It was born in 1876 and the only three surviving hunts that are older are: the Piedmont, Va., founded in 1840; the Rose Tree, Media, Pa. (1859), and the Millwood, Farmington, Mass. (1866).

The Genesee Valley Hunt is the only one in Western New York and one of two in the Upstate. There is one at Manlius near Syracuse, of recent origin.

The Hunt is one of the many picturesque squares in the distinctive pattern of life in the Valley. It gives the region about its only authentic "Merrie England" touch.

There are no red coats or pinks among the Valley riders. They wear the buff and blue of the Revolutionary army of George Washington.

European nobility, a future President of the United States and Social Registerites have ridden to hounds in the Genesee Valley. So have hundreds of plain farmers. Some of them have owned the lands across which the Hunt surges.

The father of the Genesee Valley Hunt was Maj. W. Austin Wadsworth of the Homestead. He and others had done some fox hunting prior to 1876 but there was no organization.

In 1876 Major Wadsworth, aided by Charles Carroll Fitzhugh and Judge Lockwood R. Doty, organized the Livingston County Hunt. The riders pooled their hounds of nondescript breeds. Fitzhugh died in 1878 and there was no hunting that Autumn.

The next year the club was reorganized under the name of the Genesee Valley Hunt with Major Wadsworth as president and Master of Fox Hounds. In 1880 the Major began his private pack with three hounds, Jim and Joe, and three puppies, Stubby, Speckle and Colonel, of whom the MFH once wrote:

"The last turned out useless and the former was executed for sheep murder."

The Major then began breeding his own pack of the English imported strain and for 42 years it was a private pack, owned and maintained at the Homestead by the Major. Austin Wadsworth was master until he died in 1918, nationally known as the dean of American fox hunting.

Once a letter was mailed in England, addressed to:

"W. Wadsworth, USA, the man who owns the pack of hounds."

178

It was delivered promptly.

During the Major's time, the Hunt revolved about his portly figure and his mansion, the Homestead. Socialites came there from New York and other places as Wadsworth guests for the hunting.

As Mrs. Winthrop Chanler recorded in her book, *Autumn in the Valley,* years later, "Austin Wadsworth kept a large stable of hunters and his guests were royally mounted."

Edward S. Martin, one time editor of the old *Life Magazine* attended the Hunt in 1892 and in an account of it written for *Harper's Weekly,* told of "three trains pulling in to Avon, one from Buffalo, one from Rochester and a third from New York City, full of hunting people. They took another train for Geneseo."

Martin wrote about "the people coming from Ashantee in their yellow coach, the four-in-hands from other Valley estates and the MFH in his buggy."

In those days the hounds met in front of the Big Tree Inn on Geneseo's then unpaved Main Street.

This newspaper account of the Hunt in the year 1907 breathes something of the color that surrounded it in pre-automobile times:

"From daybreak on, a steady stream of tallyhos and drags, hunting and coaching parties poured into Geneseo and drew up in front of the Big Tree Inn. Many announced their arrival a mile away with hunting horns and dazzled spectators on Main Street with their ensemble of footmen and outrunners and colorful costumes in passing four-in-hands. The Black Walnut Meadows never presented so thrilling a picture, with long lines of traps and drags, many of them gay with flags and brilliant costumes of the women."

In the 1880s the daughter of the millionaire August Bel-

179

mont of New York and her husband, Samuel Howland, established themselves on an estate in Groveland. The Howlands sponsored a horse show in Mount Morris during the fox hunting season. They decided they would have a pack and a hunt of their own. But they abandoned the idea when they found there was no place to ride to hounds in the Valley without going over Wadsworth land. The Wadsworths wanted no rival hunt club in their Valley and permission to use their lands was not forthcoming.

During the Major's long reign as MFH, some famous people rode in the Hunt, among them Theodore Roosevelt, before the turn of the century. Arthur Brisbane, the editor, who was a kinsman of the Buffalo and Batavia Carys, followed the Valley pack several times.

The Carys, a numerous tribe and all of them avid hunters, would make up an imposing cavalcade on the roads with their strings of horses, carriages, wagons and tally-ho. Others of the Buffalo social hierarchy, the Rumseys and the Hamlins, were guests at the Homestead and annual participants in the Hunt.

David Gray, the Buffalo writer, was a frequent visitor and described the Valley Hunt in a light little book, *Gallops,* which he dedicated to Arthur Brisbane and which he peopled with Valley gentry, under fictitious names.

In a later era other Buffalonians who rode to hounds in the Valley were tall Devereaux Milburn, the polo ace, and William J. Donovan, the "Wild Bill" of World War I, onetime candidate for governor of New York and head of the cloak and dagger Office of Strategic Services in the second war.

Austin Wadsworth as MFH was meticulous in his relations with Valley farmers. In English tenant leases there is a clause giving the landlord and his guests the right to ride to hounds across the rented lands. There is no such proviso in any Wadsworth lease and always the consent of the farmer has been sought before the Hunt crosses his land.

Major Wadsworth wrote what he called a Bible for the Hunt, a code of conduct for riders, which his son, William P., the present master, has recently had reprinted.

In the section titled "Of the farmer," the code proclaims:

"You have no business on a man's land but are there by his sufferance and he is entitled to every consideration. It is no excuse that you are in a hurry. It is much better for the Hunt that you should be held behind than that a farmer should be injured.

"If you take down a rail you should put it back. If you open a gate, you should shut it. If you break a fence or do any damage you cannot repair, you should report it at once to the responsible officers of the Hunt that it may be made good."

"Although you may feel convinced that it improves wheat to ride over it, the idea is not diffused or popular and the fact that some fool has gone ahead is no excuse whatever but makes the matter worse. The spectacle of a lot of men following another's track across a wheat field and killing hopelessly the young plants which the first had probably injured is too conducive of profanity to be edifying in any community."

In the section of the Hunt Bible dealing with relations with the MFH, the Major was more facetious, writing that "as a general rule he (the MFH) can enjoy your conversation and society more when not in the field with the hounds, riders, foxes and damages on his mind." To this he added:

181

"NB: The proffer of a flask is not conversation within the meaning of the above."

In dealing with the fox, the Major asked riders not to "gallop after the fox by yourself. If you caught him alone, he might bite you. Don't 'give tongue' to a woodchuck. It will cause you humiliation. There is a difference in the tails."

The code exhorts fox hunters "to keep away from the hounds at all times and at every time." The Major continued: "If you consider them worthless the Master may be quaintly indifferent to your opinion and as the quietest horse will kick at a strange dog and the stupidest dog distrusts a strange horse, KEEP AWAY."

For riders who cannot keep their mounts in check, the MFH had this blistering advice: "You had no business to bring out a horse you cannot hold any more than a biter or a kicker. If you cannot hold him, go home."

Austin Wadsworth died at the Homestead in May of 1918 in his 71st year. After his death his widow kept the Hunt going while managing the big Wadsworth estate. Maj. Gale L. Stryker was master in 1919. But the Hunt languished the next two seasons and its future was clouded.

Then a new hand took the reins. At the urging of Mrs. Austin Wadsworth and Mrs. Herbert Wadsworth, Major Winthrop Chanler became MFH and the Hunt was reorganized as a subscription pack. "Wintie" Chanler of the New York and Newport smart set had been hunting in the Valley for many years. In the early 1900s he and Mrs. Chanler bought Sweet Briar Farm, 160 acres surrounding a rambling pillared manor house, south of Geneseo near picturesque Fall Brook and on the present State Route 63.

Chanler brought from the Hudson Valley as huntsman

English-born Harry Andrews, wounded veteran of the British Life Guards in the first World War. For 30 years the Hunt and its pack were his life. He died in 1953.

While Chanler was MFH, a daughter of the house, Beatrice, was married to Pierre Allegaert in the Chapel of St. Felicitas which Mrs. Chanler, a devout Catholic, had built on the estate. The Valley never saw a wedding breakfast like theirs. To it came the Genesee Valley Hunt, huntsman, whips, hounds and all. After the breakfast the horn sounded "Boots and Saddles" and the whole party followed the pack to the covertside.

Major Chanler died in 1926 and Ernest L. Woodward, Le Roy Jello millionaire, and Jim Sam Wadsworth became joint masters of the Hunt. It was during their regime that Prince Foulke Bernadotte of the Swedish royal house and other noble Swedes rode to hounds in the Valley.

Henry W. Clune, columnist of the *Rochester Democrat and Chronicle,* recalls that on that occasion, the irrepressible Jim Sam suggested that numbers be put on the visiting royalty like football players, "so that we can identify them."

Jim Sam joined his fathers in Temple Hill Cemetery in 1930 and Woodward served as master until 1933 when he resigned. The Hunt Committee elected William P. Wadsworth, son of the founder of the Hunt, as his successor. Woodward retained his interest in the Hunt and was a liberal contributor as long as he lived. It was he who provided the sumptuous picnic lunch served free from a tent to all comers to the annual Hunt racing meets at the Kennels farm in the late 1930s.

While Bill Wadsworth was in military service from 1941 to 1945, Edward D. Mulligan, Avon gentleman farmer, was MFH. On Wadsworth's return from service, he resumed the master's post. Today he not only is master of the Hunt but its guiding spirit.

*   *   *

The years have brought changes in the Valley Hunt but its basic pattern has remained the same.

The Automotive Age has rubbed some of the glamor off the Hunt. The trains filled with Hunt-bound gentry from many places no longer steam into Avon. The four-in-hands no longer wheel up to the Big Tree Inn. One ancient tally-ho still survives and is used as the stand for the stewards and the judges at the annual racing meeting that climaxes the Hunt season.

That event, as of yore, is still highlighted by the steeple-chases, the flat race for farmers, the parade of the hounds by the MFH and staff. The site has been changed, after the sale of the traditional meeting place, the Kennels farm, to the Nations Farm of William Wadsworth. The new location is on the Nations Road, in that corner of the Valley called the Seven Nations because of the settlers of many bloods who came there in flight from the ravaged Niagara frontier in the War of 1812.

The race meeting is held on a Saturday, usually in late October or early November. On the Sunday before are held the horse trials, a major event for Valley breeders. On the night of the racing meet comes the Hunt Ball when the beauty and chivalry of the Valley gather at the Avon Inn.

The Hunt is a democratic institution. Farmers, especially those who have allowed the Hunt on their lands, are encouraged to ride, along with the landed gentry and some society folks from Rochester and Buffalo. Until recent years the farmers across whose lands the fox had been hunted were

184

given a dinner annually by the Hunt. Outsiders who have their own mounts may ride in the Hunt on payment of a fee. There is no record that they have been invited to the breakfasts at the manor houses that follow each hunt.

Essentially the Hunt is for the Valley and for Valley folks.

The season begins with cub hunting when the first tang of Autumn is felt in the September air. During October, November and sometimes into December, the Hunt meets on Saturdays at the homes of members. Traditionally the first hunt of the season starts from the Homestead.

Other places of assembly—and of the Hunt breakfasts—are Hartford House, the home of the late Senator Wadsworth; Sweet Briar, now the estate of retired Admiral Hubert Chanler, son of Winthrop; Bellwood, home of Franklin D. L. Stowe; the Charlton Farm of C. Z. Case of Avon and Edward Mulligan's farm on Barber Road, Avon. Mulligan's place is the only one without a fancy name in the English manner. Once the Hunt met at Bleak House, the Buckley mansion, but Bleak House burned. And the blue coated riders no longer gallop up the winding driveways at Ashantee as in the time of the Herbert Wadsworths.

Soon after dawn, the exact hour of the start dependent upon the condition of the ground, the sharp blast of the huntsman's horn sends the Hunt-master, huntsman, the field, horses and the pack-surging across the rolling countryside to the familiar places, the Seven Gullies, Fowlerville Bridge, Pray's Corners, Sugarberry Farm, the Black Creek Woods and McQueen's Switch.

In pre-automobile days the hunting went on until dusk. Paved roads have brought heavy motor traffic to the foxhunting country. And kennel-bred hounds, hot on the scent, have never learned to dodge automobiles when crossing roads. So nowadays the Hunt is suspended before darkness falls.

The present pack numbers 27 couples (54 dogs), about equally divided as to sexes. They are housed in new concrete kennels on a W. P. Wadsworth farm on Root's Tavern Road. For years the English breed, with a strain of whiskered Welsh, was predominant. Now most of the dogs are of the American Red Bone stock.

The present huntsman is spry, cheery, silver-haired Frank Smith, who, like his predecessor, Harry Andrews, speaks with an English accent. Smith came to the Valley from the Cheshire, Pa., Hunt.

It is a sight to watch—and hear—the pack, big-eyed and eager, flock around him when he steps into their kennels. "Down, Rapid. Down, Wealthy. Down Statesmen," he calls and he is obeyed.

Smith knows each dog by name. So do the MFH and the whips. Among the males in the pack are hounds named Joker, Justice, Salesman and Sergeant and the bitches bear such names as Wanton, Wary and Willing.

The huntsman is increasing the size of the pack by breeding. Fox hounds need plenty of exercise in the off season. The young ones have to learn all about roads, sheep, cattle, fowl and above all, they must be taught implicit obedience to the hunstman.

There are hazards in fox hunting. In 1936 ten valuable hounds were drowned crossing thin river ice. Early snowstorms have infrequently stopped the hunting. There are occasional spills at the fences. Woodchuck holes have crippled many a fine horse. That is why in the month before the season opened in 1955, Bill Wadsworth was out "breaking trails," removing branches and other obstacles and watching for other hazards.

In the old days there were "snake fences" of wood over which the hunters might vault. Wire fences, especially those barbed or electrically charged, have necessitated "made" jumps.

There is no dearth of foxes in Western New York these days of the more abundant wild life. Farmers are glad to be rid of Reynard. Even if they barred the Hunt from their acres—which they never have and probably never will—a full-fledged hunt could be run off without leaving Wadsworth land.

The Hunt brings a festive, Old World air to this rural countryside in the golden days of Autumn. Sons and daughters of the Valley hustle home for the hunting. Nowhere else in York State has the English sport flourished so long.

Some people will mourn, "The Hunt isn't what it used to be." But what is?

It may have lost some of the glitter of four-in-hand days but it is still going strong in the Valley after 80 years. And the sport itself has not changed since the Master of English Game wrote these lines four centuries ago:

"The hunting for fox is fair, for the good cry of the hounds that follow him so nigh and with so good a will. Always the scent of him while he flies through the dark wood. And he will scarcely leave a covert when he is therein; he taketh not to the open country for he trusteth not to his running, neither in his defense.

"And he will always hold to cover. When he sees that cannot last, then he goes to earth. He is so cunning and subtle that neither men nor hounds can find a remedy to keep themselves from such false turns."

Chapter 14

Red Cross Chapter No. 1

Dansville, Livingston's County largest village, lies in a spur of the Genesee Valley and in the shadow of skyscraper hills.

Out of one of those hills spurted an "All Healing Spring," which spawned a health resort known the world over. There a famous woman came to regain her broken health and it was in Dansville that Clara Barton in 1881 founded the first chapter of the Red Cross in America and unfurled the banner of mercy that flies wherever humanity is in distress.

Clarissa Harlowe Barton, born on Christmas Day of 1821 in North Oxford, Mass., was a paradoxical character. Her kinsman and biographer, William E. Barton, wrote of her that:

"She was by nature a timid woman. Her courage was the triumph of soul over instinctive shrinking from the presence of danger and the sight of pain. She achieved a superb self mastery at the stern behest of duty. It was only in things relating to herself that she ever showed embarrassment or lack of self confidence. Face to face with a great emergency, whether flood or fire or pestilence or slaughter, she completely forgot herself in the presence of the need confronting her."

She began her nursing career at the age of 11. Her brother, David, fell from the topmost rafter at a barn raising and was severely injured. For two years his sister hardly left his bedside, applying the leeches and plasters that medical science then prescribed. When David finally recovered, the long vigil had sorely taxed the vitality of the devoted sister.

At the age of 10 she saw an ox butchered and the sight affected her so that all her life she revolted at the idea of eating beef. Yet she served on the blood-bathed battlefields of three wars.

Her nature shy and shrinking, she confessed that in her early years she "knew naught but fear." Public speaking was an ordeal for her but for years she lectured all over the country before all sorts of audiences.

She taught school in New Jersey, then became a clerk in the Patent Office in Washington. When the Civil War came, she went out on the battlefields as a free-lance angel of mercy to "help feed them and bind their wounds."

In 1862 this shy spinster took command of a mule-driven army wagon with its complement of rough and profane soldiery to take provisions to Harper's Ferry. That was the forerunner of the Red Cross Motor Service of today.

After the war Clara Barton financed and originated a systematic search for soldiers missing in battle. Her health broke down after a lecture tour in the East in that cause and she sailed for Europe in 1869 under doctor's orders of "three years of absolute rest."

But she did not rest. She visited Geneva, seat of the International Red Cross, an organization which had been founded five years earlier. At Geneva she faced a barrage of questions as to why the United States had failed to sign the Treaty of Geneva which, ratified by 21 nations, would set up

190

an International Red Cross whose flag would be imumne from attack in battle and which would succor the wounded of all armies, feed the hungry of all nations.

She knew the answers. After the Civil War there prevailed in the United States a spirit of isolationism and a distrust of monarchies, coupled with the belief that the nation would never take part in another war. Friends of the Red Cross in Washington fought vainly for adherence to the Treaty.

Then in the midst of Miss Barton's "rest," the Franco-Prussian War broke out. Again she was to see the horrors of war at first hand, in the wake of the triumphant German armies. She observed also the work of the International Red Cross and on the battlefields of Europe was born in her heart a firm resolve to introduce the Red Cross to her native land.

Miss Barton made powerful friends in Europe, among them the Grand Duke and Duchess of Baden, who decorated her for her work in establishing hospitals during the Franco-Prussian War. She also received from the Emperor the Iron Cross of Germany.

In 1872 she sailed for home, afire with her project of forming a Red Cross in America. Obtaining the government's approval to the Geneva Treaty was her first objective.

But worn out by her endeavors in the European war, she suffered another physical breakdown and again Clara Barton's great work had to wait.

It came to pass that, wan and tired, she came to the historic "Water Cure" on the hill overlooking Dansville, seeking restoration of her shattered health. It was then operated by Dr. James H. Jackson and it was in the hands of the Jackson family under various names from 1858 to 1914. Since

1929 it has been the Physical Culture Hotel of the fabulous Bernarr Macfadden.

* * *

Clara Barton had been in Dansville before. She had walked into the village in 1866 during a lecture tour. For a description of that first journey from Rochester to Dansville, let's glance at her diary under date of Dec. 11, 1866:

"Rochester—took breakfast at Dr. Mandevill's. Dorr (Dorrance Atwater) came with carriage at 10. Went to the Valley Depot and thence to Avon. Waited until 12:30 and left for Wayland. Delayed some hours at Avon, arrived Wayland at 4. Took stage for Dansville at 6 P.M. Tire came off a wheel out of Dansville. Walked in, put up at American Hotel. Went to lecture at 7:30. Hall seats about 400, about full. Pleasant audience. Met Miss Dr. Austin, a pleasant lady in bloomers, and others from Water Cure. Received $50."

The Miss Dr. Austin referred to was Dr. Harriet Austin of the Water Cure staff and an adopted daughter of the then proprietor, Dr. James Caleb Jackson. She was an early advocate of dress reform for women. The Austin costume consisted of long trousers, rather than bloomers, and a Prince Albertish coat. The Water Cure's official name then was Our Hygenic Home Institute.

Miss Barton's lecture was thus described in a Dansville newspaper:

"Her lecture delivered at Canaseraga Hall on 'Work and Incidents of Army Life' was as replete with interest as her life must have been full of the hardest toil. She carried her audience with her in her mission of mercy to the soldiers and many an unbidden tear flowed from eyes unused to weeping."

When she returned to Dansville 10 years after her first visit, Miss Barton found almost immediate surcease in the serenity and beauty of the hillside resort where, she wrote, "one is not cured but is instructed how to get well."

So fond of Dansville did she become that the next year she bought a home on Health Street near the resort, a plain, two-story frame house in the shadow of a mighty hill. That house, weather beaten and in disrepair in late years, was torn down in 1955.

Her feet back on to the path of health, Clara Barton renewed her campaign for an American Red Cross. She spent long hours in her study writing letters to the right people. She made many trips to Washington but received little encouragement there from the Hayes administration. But the next President, James A. Garfield, and his secretary of state, James G. Blaine, espoused her cause.

In 1880 in the city of Washington the American Association of the Red Cross was organized with Miss Barton as its first president "for the relief of suffering in war, pestilence, famine, flood and other great national calamities."

Garfield fell under an assassin's bullet but his successor, Chester A. Arthur, proved to be a friend of the Red Cross and it was he who in 1882 signed the treaty binding the United States to the International Red Cross.

At last Clara Barton's major battle had been won. From Dansville she had called upon America to break its shell of provincial insularity and America had answered the call.

*　　*　　*

Even before the adherence of the American government to the Treaty of Geneva, Miss Barton and her associates had

193

been busy on the home front in Dansville, drafting plans for a local branch.

Some of the first meetings of the little group of neighbors were held in the apothecary shop of "Doctor" Gottlob Bastian, one of the leaders of the movement, because the druggist found it difficult to leave his store.

Today a prized possession in the Dansville chapter house is a fine, hand-made walnut desk which belonged to the "doctor" and upon which the preliminary plans for the first Red Cross unit in America were drafted. Mrs. Carl E. Bastian, widow of a grandson of the apothecary of 1881, recently presented it to Clara Barton Red Cross Chapter No. 1.

The files of the *Dansville Advertiser* relate that on Aug. 1 "a small but select company of our citizens . . . assembled in the pleasant parlors of Miss Clara Barton's residence, to hear from her eloquent lips some facts respecting the origin, present condition and prospects of the society of the Red Cross."

At that meeting a call was issued for a public meeting to be held the next Sabbath evening, August 7, in the Presbyterian Church to—"if the way seems open, make arrangements for a more formal meeting at which there shall be established a local organization, auxiliary to the national society of the Red Cross."

Clara Barton addressed that rally in the Presbyterian Church and the response was so enthusiastic that 15 days later, on August 22, 1881, in St. Paul's Lutheran Church America's first local Red Cross society was formally organized with a membership of 57.

In the beginning the organization was called the Dansville Society of the Red Cross. When it was reorganized in the first World War, it was renamed the Southern Livingston County Chapter. After that war, by special permission of national headquarters, it took its logical name, Clara Barton Chapter No. 1.

The new chapter was hardly a month old before it found work to do. There was a terrible forest fire in Michigan and Miss Barton's home was converted into relief headquarters. Its rooms were filled with supplies. Boxes were stamped with the seal of the Red Cross and sent away. A fund of $3,000 was hastily raised in the Dansville region and Major Mark Bunnell of the village was dispatched to Michigan as agent for the chapter. Thus he was the first field representative of the American Red Cross in any disaster area.

In the Clara Barton Chapter House is a time-worn flag with the familiar crimson cross on a field of white. That banner flew from the masthead of the first Red Cross relief boat to ply American waters.

With Miss Barton aboard, the *John V. Throop* in March of 1884 made two round trips between Cairo, Ill., and Cincinnati during the Ohio River floods. In April relief work shifted to the Mississippi Valley where the same little flag flew from the *Mattie Bell* on her mercy voyage from St. Louis to New Orleans and return, with Clara Barton again in command.

The historic flag was presented Clara Barton Chapter by the founder's grandniece, Mrs. Stephen Butler, at the celebration of the 50th anniversary of the founding of the chapter in Dansville on Sept. 9, 1931.

Miss Barton was instrumental in forming the second local chapter in the nation in October of 1881. It was in Rochester and Susan B. Anthony, the crusader for women's rights, another gallant spinster, sounded the call for members. Soon a third chapter was organized in Syracuse and the American Red Cross was on its way.

In 1886 Clara Barton bade farewell to Dansville at a gathering of neighbors in these moving words:

"Your pretty town has given me back my strength. To the rest of your valleys and the strength of your hills I am grateful . . . and in this parting from Dansville and its citizens, my beloved neighbors, the best love of my heart is wounded and come weal or woe, from now to the end, I shall remember."

After that the story of Miss Barton's life until her resignation in 1904 as president of the American Red Cross is essentially the story of the organization she mothered. The major disasters kept coming, floods, cyclones, famines, earthquakes and pestilence, and in 1898 the Spanish-American War that took Clara Barton, aged 76, to Cuba and the front.

Even after her retirement as head of the Red Cross, the gentle old lady was incessantly active. Her biographer wrote: "Even to those who were near her, she never seemed to grow old. At ninety there was no mark of physical infirmity upon her. . . ."

The end came for Clarissa Harlowe Barton at the age of 90 in her winter home at Glen Echo, Md., on Easter Sunday of the year 1912. The mother of the Red Cross sleeps near her birthplace at North Oxford, Mass. That girlhood home was purchased by the Unitarian Church women of America and is a public shrine.

* * *

Nor has Dansville, "the pretty town that gave me back my strength," forgotten Clara Barton.

Her memory is enshrined in the name of the Clara Barton Chapter No. 1 and in the chapter house on Elizabeth Street are the flag of the flood relief boats, the apothecary's ancient desk and other keepsakes of the early days.

There is a state historical marker in front of St. Paul's Lutheran Church where the first Red Cross Chapter was formed and the street on which the church faces has recently been renamed Clara Barton Street by the village fathers. It used to be Exchange Street. Near that short street also stands the Presbyterian Church where was held the preliminary public meeting that led to the organization of the pioneer chapter. Dansville people believe there is no other street named after Clara Barton in the United States.

September 9, 1931 was a red letter day in Dansville history. The natural amphitheater of scenic Stony Brook State Park south of the village was jammed with thousands.

Escorted by the Cavalry troop that was the Genesee Valley's own, Gov. Franklin D. Roosevelt came to pay tribute to Clara Barton on the golden anniversary of the American Red Cross. James W. Wadsworth, the former Senator, was another speaker and President Hoover gave a nation-wide salute—by radio.

Come weal or woe, America remembers Clara Barton.

She is remembered wherever waves the white banner with the crimson cross, amid the cries of dying men on battle fields, amid the rubble of ruined cities and the roar of the flood waters, wherever humanity is in distress, wherever the dread Four Horsemen ride.

It was in the Genesee Country that first the oriflamme of mercy was unfurled on this continent.

Chapter 15

"The Cowled Farmers"

On a sunny day the traveler on the Avon-Geneseo high-road sees off in the Valley to the West a sheen like that of shining waters.

Should he follow the gleam, he would find himself on the North River Road in the Township of York, one mile north-west of Piffard, where a row of new, low buildings crowns a little ridge. It was the roofs of those buildings that he had seen shining in the distance.

He sees men in robes and cowls, some in brown, some in white, many with shaven heads and bearded faces, working around the grounds and in the fields, building a barn, tending cattle, doing all manner of manual tasks—all in utter silence.

The traveler rubs his eyes. Is this the familiar Genesee Valley of the fox-hunting squires, the land that was settled by Connecticut Yankees or is this a little corner of the Old World in a medieval time?

He has come to the Trappist-Cistercian Abbey of Our Lady of the Genesee.

It was in April, 1951, that the first "Cowled Farmers," a little band of six, came to the river valley to establish there the twelfth of their monasteries in North America and the first in New York State.

The order, whose full name is the Cistercians of the Strict Observance, goes back nearly 500 years to 1068 when it was founded in Citeaux, France, to revive the Rule of St. Benedict, which was based on the ideals of poverty, humiliation, separation from the world, simplicity of life, manual toil, litugical praise and spiritual reading.

The name Trappist comes from the Abbey of La Trappe in Normandy where the Abbe de Rance restored the rigid regimen which had become relaxed in the 17th Century.

Sacrifice of all worldly pleasures, even comforts, along with seclusion and silence are the essence of the Trappist way of life. Isolated sites are sought for monasteries. The monks never converse with one another, except when it is imperative. Otherwise they use, again only when it is necessary, a sign language which is ten centuries old. Not only do they abstain from speech but they avoid making any noise that would disturb the calm of the cloister, such as slamming of doors or walking with heavy feet.

Trappists are not allowed to eat meat unless they are ill. Fish and eggs are taboo. The usual meal consists of soup, vegetables, whole wheat, coffee and bread. Milk and cheese are occasional additions to their menu.

They sleep, fully clad, except for their shoes, a prescribed seven hours on hard straw pellets laid on boards. They arise at 2 o'clock in the morning to chant the Divine Office, the official prayers of the church, from their choir stalls.

Devotions, contemplation and at least four hours of manual labor, even for the choir monks, made up the average Trappist day. There is no work on Sundays or on major fast days. For them there are no newspapers, no secular magazines, no movies, no radio, no television, no games. They receive infrequent visits from their families, restricted to three days at a time. They may write letters only four times a year and then only to near relatives.

They live in a world of their own, a world of silent abnegation and prayer, the world of St. Bernard in the medieval heyday of the Cistercian Order.

The beginnings of Our Lady of the Genesee were humble indeed. The first half dozen monks were soon joined by the late Rt. Rev. M. Gerard McGinley, then prior and the first abbot. Father Gerard had served at Gethsemani since 1926. There he had been confessor to Thomas Merton, whose books on Trappist life, notably *The Seven-Story Mountain*, have been widely read.

Father Gerard brought with him from Kentucky the traditional plain wooden cross of the Cistercians, and when the colony numbered 33, the monastery was formally founded on May 26, 1951.

The pioneer "Cowled Farmers" lived for three weeks in one of the Valley manor houses, stately Westerly, the summer residence of Porter Chandler. It is an historic house. On one of its window panes a former First Lady long ago scratched her name with a ring. It is still there.

The name on the pane is "Julia G. Tyler." The widow of the tenth President had come to Westerly in 1871 to care for the mistress of the mansion, her daughter Julia, the wife of William H. Spencer, Jr., of a pioneer Valley family. That daughter died a few hours after she had given birth to a girl. The house caught fire and she and her babe were carried out. The blaze was quickly extinguished but Julia Spencer died from shock. Her mother never came back to the Valley.

Probably John Tyler's widow scratched her name on the window in a moment of lonely abstraction. The Genesee

Valley was a quiet place for one used to the glitter of Washington and Virginia society.

Porter Chandler inherited Westerly, the home of his mother who was a daughter of Charles F. Wadsworth. Wadsworth, a son of the Civil War general, James S. Wadsworth, raised thoroughbred short-horn cattle on the estate.

Nearby was old York Landing, a busy shipping point in early river and Genesee Valley Canal days. Underlying the whole area is a bed of salt and salt wells have been drilled near the monastery site. Only three miles to the southwest is the Retsof rock salt mine, said to be the largest in the world.

Getting back to the Trappists and the 20th Century, the 580 acres which Chandler presented to the order were known as the Harris farm. The Trappists purchased the Sherwood farm of 450 acres, site of the present monastery, and the adjoining farm, once the property of Troop M of the old First Cavalry. The old troop farmhouse, according to Valley lore, once was the scene of lively cock fights. Now it is the women's guest house of the abbey and is known as Nazareth Place.

At first the monks held their services in the little white St. Raphael's Mission Church in Piffard. Then they moved into a century-old house on the Harris farm which had been an inn. They renamed it Bethlehem Place.

Its crowded quarters were remodeled to fit the monks' needs. Chickens were chased from the second floor to provide a dormitory. A chapel was established. There were already barns, two silos, a garage and other farm buildings on the place. But there was no livestock, no farming equipment.

That lack was soon remedied. One day an Elmira man drove a truck into the yard and unloaded a Holstein cow, two pigs and 50 chickens, the little colony's first livestock.

Today it has a herd of 50 milking cows, besides young stock. For a time it raised a pedigreed strain of pigs but has gone back to "standard" stock. Trappist animals have won blue ribbons at the Caledonia Fair and at the State Fair in Syracuse.

In the Trappists' early days in the Valley, a stranger drove a used truck into the yard at Bethlehem Place, walked up to Father Gerard, handed him the keys and a bill of sale and after saying, "maybe you can use this truck," departed without giving his name. He had driven the vehicle from New York City.

Other gifts poured in—clothing, food, furnishings, farm tools, cash. The monks began baking on a small stove in a shed a few loaves of their famous bread made from their own formula. Now they turn out 2,000 loaves a day in a modern bakery, to which an addition is being erected. Monks' bread is in heavy demand in Rochester, Buffalo and nearby places, as well as in New York, Cleveland and distant points. It vies with the raising of wheat and milk production as the abbey's richest sources of revenue.

In June, 1951, work was begun on the present buildings on the old Sherwood farm. The first unit completed was the Gate House of brick, which is linked by passageways to three other steel-frame buildings with exteriors and roofs of galvanized, corrugated steel—which shine in the sunlight. They house cloister, church, two cubicled dormitories, chapter room, dental hygiene office, kitchen, refectory, bakery, infirmary and other units. The present chapel, impressive in its simple dignity, was dedicated in the Spring of 1953.

The design and furnishings of the abbey are as austere as the lives of its residents. No woman is ever allowed beyond the reception room of the Gate House.

Most of the construction was done by the monks themselves. There are carpenters and construction workers among them and others who had been bookkeepers and salesmen learned something of the builder's trade. In the Fall of 1955 a cement-block addition to the bakeshop and a large cow barn were under construction.

There are currently 72 residents at Our Lady of the Genesee, including 12 priests. The remainder of the population is divided about equally between the choir monks, who wear white, and the lay brothers in their rough brown habits.

The lay brothers come from all corners of the nation, along with some from Hawaii and China. They come from every walk of life, every calling. One brother was a seismologist and is fascinated by the rocks of the Genesee Country. Only two of the brothers are over 50. Most of them are in their twenties and thirties and many of them are war veterans.

In the monastic community there are no distinctions. Everyone sleeps in the same quarters, eats the same food, wears clothing of the same quality. No Trappist has any possessions of his own.

Only unmarried men over 15 years of age are admitted into the order. Candidates who are accepted after a trial period spend a month or two in secular garb before beginning a two-year novitiate. At the end of five years solemn and binding vows are made. Not all complete the period of the novitiate. Some find the regimen too rigorous.

On Nov. 9, 1953, Rochester's Cathedral of the Sacred Heart, a few blocks from the Genesee, was the scene of ancient ritual which elevated Our Lady of the Genesee from a monastery to an abbey and blessed Father Gerard as its first abbot. The ceremony, first of its kind held in Rochester, brought high church dignitaries and the white-robed choir monks and the lay brothers in their brown habits and shaven heads attracted much attention.

Twenty-three months later, the monks came up from the Valley again for another service in the Rochester cathedral. This time they came with sadness in their hearts. Their abbot was dead, stricken with a heart attack in France, and they came to attend the solemn pontifical mass for their beloved leader.

Now the abbot sleeps in the little abbey cemetery in The Valley. Death came while he was attending a conclave of the Trappists at the mother house of the order in Citeaux, France.

Only ten days before he sailed, I had talked with him in his tiny cluttered office where he worked and slept. It was my first meeting with Father Gerard and my first visit to the abbey.

That day the slender, smiling 49-year-old abbot spoke with almost boyish enthusiasm of his coming trip abroad. He told of his plans, already well advanced, for a fine new monastery beside the Genesee. He planned to visit monasteries in the Old World and gather some ideas. He said he hoped that ground would be broken for the new structure at Piffard within two years and that it could be completed within five years. At that time the actual site of the new monastery had not been selected.

Now others must carry out his dream. His death has cast a pall over the cloistered community. The Valley will miss the sincere and serene priest who had won a cordial reception for the Trappists in a countryside that is predominantly Protestant.

There are many visitors to the monastery, sometimes as

many as 300 on a pleasant Sunday. Priests and laymen from a wide area come for retreats. Often there are 40 in the Guest House.

The Trappists now have 1,600 acres of good farm land. Three streams, the Genesee, the Salt River and Beard's Creek, cross it. So do two railroads, the Pennsylvania, in the old canal bed, and the Genesee & Wyoming, known as "the Gee Whiz," which hauls salt from the big rock salt mine at Retsof to Caledonia.

The added land has been acquired as a protection against undesirable encroachments. The seclusion of other abbeys has been disturbed by such neighbors as night clubs, race tracks and industrial plants. The Trappists aim to preserve the tranquil isolation of Our Lady of the Genesee.

In four short years the Cistercians of the Strict Observance have accomplished much in the Valley. There are the buildings on the hill and the monks laboring in silence on land over which in other Autumns the blue-clad riders of the Genesee Valley Hunt surged in pursuit of the sly fox.

Their bells echoing across the Valley proclaim that there still is a frontier, even in this age of the jet and the jitters. In mid-20th Century the Valley has received a new band of pioneers, "the Cowled Farmers," who came carrying the Cross as did the black-robed Jesuits three centuries before them.

The monks take their place at the end of a long line of historical settlers—the Senecas, the White Woman of the Genesee, the white pioneers handy with ax and gun; the landed gentry, the emigrants who dug the canals and built the railroads, peoples of many bloods and many ways.

The Trappists have brought to the many-sided land of the

Genesee still another way of life. In one corner of the old Indian valley, the clock has been turned back and a bit of the Old World and the Middle Ages lives again.

THE END

A CARD OF THANKS

I am grateful to all those who helped me gather the material for this book. Particularly I would like to acknowledge the valuable assistance and suggestions given me by Mrs. Marie Preston, Livingston County Historian, and her secretary, Miss Ann Patchett, during the many hours I spent in the Livingston County Historian Center in Geneseo.

My thanks also go to Mrs. Katherine Carmer Bailey of the Wadsworth Library, William P. Wadsworth and Reverdy Wadsworth of Geneseo; J. Frederick Beuerlein of Mount Morris, Gordon W. Harvey, general manager of the Genesee State Park Commission, James Mack of Portageville, Cal De Golyer of Castile, Mrs. Ruth Brown, Leicester Town Historian; Reid Parker of Perry, William D. Conklin of Dansville, Henry R. Seldon of Avon, Arthur Donnan, York town historian and Stephen J. Fitzgerald of Rochester.

Also I found Sherman Peer's book, *Genesee River Country,* a mine of information on the history and legends of the Genesee Valley. The same is true of *Historical Wyoming,* the monthly publication whose chief editor is Wyoming County Historian Harry S. Douglass.